Canadian Provinces and Territories

Grades 4-6

Written by Ruth Solski
Illustrated by S&S Learning Material

ISBN 1-55035-663-1
Canadian Provinces and Territories, SSJ1-38
Copyright 2000 S&S Learning Materials
Revised December 2003
15 Dairy Avenue
Napanee, Ontario
K7R 1M4
All Rights Reserved * Printed in Canada
A Division of the Solski Group

Published in Canada by:
S&S Learning Materials
15 Dairy Avenue
Napanee, Ontario
K7R 1M4
www.sslearning.com

Published in the United States by:
T4T Learning Materials
3909 Witmer Road PMB 175
Niagara Falls, New York
14305
www.t4tlearning.com

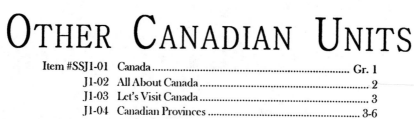

Look For OTHER CANADIAN UNITS

Published by:
S&S Learning Materials
15 Dairy Avenue
Napanee, Ontario
K7R 1M4

Distributed in U.S.A. by:
T4T Learning Materials
3909 Witmer Road PMB 175
Niagara Falls, New York
14305

© S&S Learning Materials

2

SSJ1-38

 # Canadian Provinces and Territories

Table of Contents

CANADIAN PROVINCES AND TERRITORIES

Expectations

Students will:

- describe the physical features of regions within the provinces and territories.
- identify how regions are interdependent in relationship to their economies and governments.
- demonstrate and become aware of the various relationships economically and culturally, etc. within and between Canadian regions.
- identify the characteristics of the physical regions of their individual province/territory and all of Canada.
- name and describe the main features of a river system.
- demonstrate an understanding of the significance of the St. Lawrence River and the Great Lakes systems.
- identify their individual province/territory's major natural resources and their uses.
- identify Canada's major natural resources and their uses.
- identify and describe types of communities in each physical region of each province and territory.
- demonstrate an understanding of the exchange of products within each province or territory and throughout Canada.
- identify the physical regions of Canada.
- describe and compare the physical environments of these regions according to land forms.
- identify the natural resources used to create Canadian products and the provinces/territories from which they originate.
- use appropriate vocabulary to describe their inquiries and observations.
- construct and read a wide variety of graphs, charts, diagrams, maps and models for specific purposes such as to determine physical features, area of regions, size of population, climate, etc.
- locate and label provinces, territories and capital cities within each region on a map of Canada.
- identify Ottawa as the capital of Canada.
- locate and label the Great Lakes and other major bodies of water and waterways in Canada.
- identify symbols used to outline boundaries (international, national, provincial).
- locate and label the physical regions of Canada on a map.
- use cardinal and intermediate directions, non-pictorial symbols and colour on a map to locate and describe physical regions.

List of Resources

1. **Discover Canada Series**: Grolier Limited, Toronto. This is an excellent series of books. Each book is up-to-date, well laid out and contains interesting information and wonderful photographs

2. **Hello Canada Series**: Lerner Publications. This series is easier to read and follow. It is an excellent series for students who have reading difficulties at higher grade levels. The books are laid out well and information is easy to find. The photographs are colourful and contain visual information as well.

3. Greenwood, Barbara. The Kids Book of Canada. Kids Can Press, Toronto.

4. Harris, Jeanette. Canada - the land and its people. Macdonald Education, England.

5. Lynn, Janet/Moore, Christopher. The Story of Canada. Lester Publishing Limited.

6. Colby, Dulcie; Harrison, John; Kerr, Carol. Canada is .... Music (Grade 3-4). Gordon V. Thompson Limited, Toronto.

7. Colby, Dulcie; Harrison, John; Kerr, Carol. Canada is..... Music (Grade 5-6). Gordon V. Thompson Limited, Toronto.

Teacher Input Suggestions

1. **Planning Ahead:**
   Locate any of the following items. Also send an information sheet home requesting any souvenirs, postcards, photographs, books, labels from Canadian products or items that the student could contribute to the topic that they are studying.

   Canadian atlases; reference books on Canada; reference books on the individual provinces and territories; travel brochures and pamphlets; travel posters about Canada and Canadian places; road maps of the various provinces and territories; wall maps of the world, North America, Canada; pictures of tourist attractions across Canada; pictures of different types of communities found in Canada; photographs of different ethnic people to show the students that Canada is a multi-cultural nation; pictures of each provincial and territorial coat of arms, flag, floral emblem, animal, bird; postcards of different places located in Canada; pictures of Canada's capital city and the Prime Minister; puzzles of Canada

2. **Introduction:**
   - Decorate your classroom door with Canadian flags, maple leaves and a large sign that says **WELCOME TO CANADA!** On the either side of the door display a full size R.C.M.P. standing guard. On the inside of the door display labelled pictures of Canada, songs and poetry.
   - Play Canada's National Anthem, **O Canada**, and sing the words. On a chart display the words and discuss what they mean. Teach your own provincial/territorial song if there is one.
   - Show a film or video that provides an overview of Canada from coast to coast. Discuss the film with your students. Show a film or video on your own province/territory if possible.
   - Brainstorm with your students facts that they know about Canada. List the facts on the chalkboard or on a chart.
   - Brainstorm with your students questions they would like to have answered about Canada. Record their questions on a chart leaving a space below each question for its answer. Answers will appear throughout the topic. Record them under each question.

3. **Bulletin Board Displays:**
   - Locate a large map of Canada. Display it on a bulletin board. Pin one end of a piece of string to each province and territory. Attach the other end to the bulletin board outside the map area. Make name cards for all the provinces and territories. Have the students practise naming them by pinning the name card at the end of each piece of string.
   - Laminate a large, blank, political map of Canada that shows the divisions and borders of the various provinces and territories. The map should show the position of each capital city. The students may use a water-soluble pen to mark the names of the provinces and territories and their capital cities.
   - Display pictures of famous tourist attractions around a large map of Canada. Connect each picture with string to its location in Canada. The pictures should be labelled.
   - Around a large map display pictures of various communities found in Canada. Use large paper arrows to show where the communities are located.

4. **Music Ideas:**
   - Teach your class songs that pertain to Canada and the different provinces.
   - Listen to Canadian folk music and popular music sung by Canadian artists.
   - Incorporate ethnic music if you live in a multicultural part of Canada.

5. **Art Ideas:**
   - The students may paint a mural to show different types of communities located in Canada.
   - Individual pictures of places in Canada may be painted, crayoned or chalked.
   - Collages may be made using pictures of different parts of Canada.
   - Post cards may be designed displaying tourist attractions found in Canada.

Canadian Provinces and Territories

6. **Organization of the Unit:**
   - This unit has been divided into Lesson Plans with reproducible follow-ups. Each lesson may need to be adapted or the ideas may be used to design your own lesson plans in order to suit the needs of your own student.

Lesson Plans

Lesson #1: Where is Canada?

Expectations:
The students will:

- identify, locate and label the continents and oceans of the world.
- identify Canada's location in the world.
- recall and record learned information.

Discussion Time:
Using a wall map or a globe explain to the students that the world is made up of large land masses and large bodies of water. The land masses are divided into seven continents and the water is divided into four oceans. Locate the continents one at a time on the map of the world. Discuss their size, shape, location and the countries involved in each one. Record the name of each continent on a chart or the chalkboard. Beside each one record its size in square kilometres. *Asia - 44 008 000 sq. km; Africa - 30 253 000 sq. km; North America - 24, 211, 000 sq. km; South America - 17 833 000 sq. km; Antarctica - 14 000 000 sq. km; Europe -10 445 000 sq. km; Australia - 7 713 000 sq. km. Star the continent that is the largest. The continents may then be numbered according to size from the largest to the smallest.

Locate the various oceans. Record their names on a chart or chalkboard. Beside each one record its size. Pacific Ocean - 181 000 000 sq. km; Atlantic Ocean - 94 000 000 sq. km; Indian Ocean - 74 000 000 sq. km; Arctic Ocean - 13 986 000 sq. km.

Have the students locate Canada on a wall map of the world. Discuss the continent that Canada is found in. What are the names of two other countries found in the same continent? (United States, Mexico)

Follow-ups:
1. Reproduce Map #1 entitled **"Continents of the World"** (page 36). On the map the students are to locate and label the seven continents and four oceans. They are to locate and colour Canada red.

2. Reproduce Worksheet #1 entitled **"Where is Canada?"** (page 13). The students are to complete the sheet by recording the correct answers on the lines.

Lesson #2: Canada's Borders

Expectations:
The students will:

- identify Canada's borders within the country.
- identify and label Canada's borders.
- recall and record learned information.

Discussion Time:
Use a large wall map of Canada to show the country and bodies of water that border it. Have the students locate Alaska and the United States. Locate the bodies of water that border Canada. They are: Hudson Bay, Arctic Ocean, Atlantic Ocean, Pacific Ocean.

Follow-ups:
1. Reproduce Map #2 entitled **"Canada's Borders"** (page 37). On the map have the students trace in green the border lines of Canada. Print the names of the bodies of water and the country that borders Canada. With a red pencil crayon the students may then trace the border lines that divide Canada into provinces and territories.

2. Reproduce Worksheet #2 entitled **"Canada's Borders"** (page 14). The students will read each activity and complete it neatly and accurately.

Lesson #3: Canada's Provinces and Territories

Expectations:
The students will:

- identify and locate each territory and province found in Canada.
- label each province and territory correctly on a map of Canada.
- identify the provinces called Atlantic Provinces, Prairie Provinces, and the Territories.
- identify their own province or territory.

Discussion Time:
Point to a wall map of Canada and explain that Canada is divided into thirteen different land areas that are called provinces and territories. Pose the following questions. "Who can locate and name the province in which we live?" "Can someone find another province or territory and tell us its name?" Once all the provinces and territories are located, have the students identify the provinces by using a compass rose.

Example: Which province is to the west of Ontario? (Manitoba) Which province is east of Alberta? (Saskatchewan).

Follow-ups:
1. Reproduce Map #3 entitled **"Canada's Provinces and Territories"** (page 38). Place the same map on an overhead. Working from the Atlantic Coast to the Pacific Coast have the students name and label each province neatly by printing in the rectangle provided. Then have the students label the territories. The students will colour each province and territory a different colour.

2. Reproduce Worksheet #3 entitled **"Canada's Provinces and Territories"** (page 15). The students will record the required answers on the worksheet.

Lesson #4: Borders Inside Canada

Expectations:
The students will:

- use a map to locate information.
- identify and complete borders between provinces.
- label a political outline map of Canada independently.

Discussion:
The students will use their labelled political map of Canada to locate the answers to the following questions.
1. Which two provinces share the shortest border? (***New Brunswick and Nova Scotia***)
2. Which province has its border entirely surrounded by salt water? (***Prince Edward Island***)
3. Which provinces border on Hudson Bay? (***Manitoba, Ontario, Québec***)
4. Which province borders the Pacific Ocean? (***British Columbia***)
5. Which province's northern border is found on Nunavut? (***Manitoba***)
6. Which provinces share their southern border with the United States? Name them east to west. (***New Brunswick, Québec, Ontario, Manitoba, Saskatchewan, Alberta, British Columbia***)
7. Which territory shares its western border with the Northwest Territories? (***Nunavut***)
8. Which territory shares its borders with Alaska and British Columbia? (***Yukon Territory***)
9. Which province shares its eastern border with Québec and its western border with Manitoba? (***Ontario***)
10. Which province shares its borders with Québec and the Atlantic Ocean? (***Newfoundland & Labrador***)
11. Which two provinces do not have borders on any ocean? (***Alberta, Saskatchewan***)

12. Which province has borders on fresh water and salt water? (*Ontario*)

13. Which two provinces have the Ottawa River as a border? (*Ontario, Québec*)

Follow-ups:

1. Reproduce Map #4 entitled **"Borders Inside Canada"** (page 39). Have the students complete the broken borders found on the map. Then have them practise labelling the provinces. This activity may be repeated many times until the students become quite proficient recalling the borders and names of the provinces and territories.

2. Reproduce Worksheet #4 entitled **"Border Riddles"** (page 16). The students will read the riddle and locate the province or territory on a map, then record its name on the line at the end of the riddle.

3. Reproduce Worksheet #5 entitled **"Search for Each Province/Territory and Its Capital City"** (page 17). The students are to locate and circle the names of the provinces and territories with red. The names of the capital cities are to be circled with green.

Lesson #5: Canada's Capital Cities

Expectations:
The students will:

- identify and locate each capital city on a map.
- associate each capital city to its province or territory.
- associate each province and territory to its two-digit designator.

Discussion Time:

A) Using a wall map or a political map of Canada found in an atlas, locate the capital city of each province and territory with your students. Draw attention to the legend or key to find out how a capital city is marked on a map. Work from the east coast to the west and then north. On the chalkboard or a chart, list the names of the provinces and territories. Beside each one write the capital city as the students locate it.

Example:

Province	Capital City	Designator

New Brunswick - Fredericton; Québec - Québec City; Ontario - Toronto; Capital City of Newfoundland & Labrador - St. John's; Prince Edward Island - Charlottetown; Nova Scotia - Halifax; Canada - Ottawa; Manitoba - Winnipeg; Saskatchewan - Regina; Alberta - Edmonton; British Columbia - Victoria; Yukon - Whitehorse; Northwest Territories - Yellowknife; Nunavut - Iqaluit

B) Explain to the students that each province and territory has a provincial capital; as well, the country has a national capital called "Ottawa". Each capital city is the place where the provincial government meets and the national capital city is where the federal government meets. Each province also has a two-digit designator. Record the designator on the chart as well. The designator has replaced the abbreviated forms used years ago.

Alberta - AB; British Columbia - BC; Manitoba - MB; New Brunswick - NB; Newfoundland & Labrador - NF; Northwest Territories - NT; Nova Scotia - NS; Nunavut - NT; Ontario - ON; Prince Edward Island - PE; Québec - QC; Saskatchewan - SK; Yukon Territory - YT; Nunavut - NU

Follow-ups:

1. Reproduce Map #5 entitled **"Canada's Capital Cities"** (page 40). Students will record the name of each capital city on the line or in the box neatly. Underline the name of the capital city of Canada in red.

2. Reproduce Worksheet #6 entitled **"Let's Research Canada"** (page 18). The students will use reference materials to locate the answers to the questions about the provinces, territories and their capital cities. They will record their findings on the line after each question.

CANADIAN PROVINCES AND TERRITORIES

Lesson #6: The Physical Regions of Canada

Expectations:

The students will:

- identify the characteristics of the physical regions of Canada.
- be able to locate the physical regions on a map of Canada.
- understand and use geographical terminology.

Discussion Time:

List the following geographical terms on the chalkboard or on chart paper. Discuss each term with your students. Beside each one write its meaning. Complete the activity as a chart. Have the students make their own chart using the same headings and terms. The terms and meanings may be copied onto their charts.

Geographical Terms

Term	Meaning
1. bay	a large, wide, deeply curved inlet along a coastline
2. coastline	the outline of a coast
3. fiord	a long, narrow bay of the sea bordered by steep cliffs
4. glacier	a large mass of ice formed from snow on high ground that moves slowly down a mountain or along a sloping valley or spreading slowly over a large area of land until it melts or breaks up
5. inlet	a narrow strip of water running from a larger body of water into the land or between islands
6. island	a body of land completely surrounded by water
7. lake	a sizeable body of fresh or salt water surrounded by land
8. lowland	a low, flat region
9. mountain	a very high hill
10. peak	the pointed top of a mountain or hill
11. peninsula	a piece of land almost surrounded by water
12. plain	a flat stretch of land; prairie
13. plateau	a large high plain found near mountains
14. river	a large natural stream of water that flows into a lake, an ocean, or another river
15. sea level	the surface of the sea; land forms and ocean beds are measured as so many metres above or below sea level
16. tundra	a large region of treeless land between the permanent polar ice and the northern forests
17. valley	an area of low-lying land between mountains or hills; often has a river or stream flowing through it

Reproduce the Information Sheet #1 entitled **"The Physical Regions of Canada"** (pages 45 to 48) for students to read or use them to make overheads or for your own general knowledge to use in teaching the topic. On the chalkboard or a chart, list the seven physical regions found in Canada. Explain to your students that the physical features of a country affect the way people live and work.

Locate each region one at a time on a wall map. Have the students read the information for each region. Discuss the following items: location; land forms; minerals; vegetation; wildlife. After all the regions have been located and discussed, give your students the reproducible Worksheet #7 (page 19) entitled **"Physical Regions of Canada"**. Make the same chart on the chalkboard. The students will review each physical region and record the necessary information on the chart.

Follow-Ups:

Reproduce Map #6 entitled **"The Physical Regions of Canada"** (page 41). The students will label the physical regions by recording each region's name in the empty box.

CANADIAN PROVINCES AND TERRITORIES

Lesson # 7: Rivers and Lakes of Canada

Expectations:

The students will:
- identify and describe the main features of a river system.
- identify and locate major lakes and rivers of Canada.
- demonstrate an understanding of the significance of the St. Lawrence River and the Great Lakes System.
- understand the terms *mouth, source, branch, delta, flow, tributary,* etc.

A) Rivers of Canada:

Discussion Time:

Reproduce Information Sheet #2 entitled **"What is a River?"** (pages 49 to 50) for your students to read or use them to make overheads. Read the information with the students and discuss the following terms. Record the terms on the chalkboard or a chart. Have the students give a meaning for each term. The students may copy the terms and their meanings on their own chart.

River Terms

Terms	Meanings
1. river	a large body of flowing water that moves over the land in a long channel
2. source of a river	the beginning of a river usually found in the mountains
3. headwaters	small streams found at the beginning of a river
4. rills	tiny, narrow channels of flowing water
5. brooks	wider and deeper channels of flowing water
6. streams	made from brooks joining together
7. tributaries	all the rills, brooks and streams that carry water to a river
8. river system	of a river and all its tributaries
9. drainage basin	the area of land that a river system drains
10. Continental Divide	an imaginary line in the Rocky Mountains that divides North America into two large drainage basins
11. river channel	the land on either side of and beneath the flowing water
12. river bed	the bottom of the channel
13. river banks	the sides of the channel
14. waterfalls	a steep drop in the river's channel caused by erosion
15. rapids	water tumbling over large boulders
16. canyon	a deep channel with high walls cut by a fast flowing river
17. flood plain	a flat area found on one or both sides of the banks of a river, covered by water during a flood
18. meander	a snake-like bend in a river
19. mouth of a river	the place where the river empties its waters into another body of water
20. delta	dirt and rock left by a river at its mouth to form a body of land
21. river's load	dirt and rock that the river carries as it travels to its mouth

Follow-Ups:

1. Reproduce Map #7 entitled **"The Rivers of Canada"** (page 42) for each student or use it to make an overhead for student viewing. The students are to locate the names of rivers on the map. Have them trace in blue each river that they find. Discuss the sizes and locations of as many rivers as you can.

2. Reproduce Worksheet #8 entitled **"Important Rivers of Canada"** (page 20). The students are to complete the worksheet using Map #7 entitled **"The Rivers of Canada"** (page 42).

3. Reproduce Worksheet #9 entitled **"How Long Are The Rivers of Canada?"** (page 21). The students are to arrange and record on the chart the names of the rivers in the order of size, from the largest to the smallest.

B) Lakes of Canada:

Discussion Time:

Reproduce the Information Sheet #3 entitled **"What is a Lake?"** (page 51) or use it to make an overhead. The students will read the sheet and then locate the answers to the following questions:

1. Define a lake. (***a body of water surrounded by land***)

2. How were most lakes formed? (***glaciers carved deep valleys that filled up with water***)

3. From where do lakes get their water? (***fed by rivers and streams, underground springs or streams***)

4. Why are lakes important to communities? (***provide trade and travel; water used to irrigate farmers' fields; supply water to communities; generate electricity; used for recreation***)

5. Why are the Great Lakes famous? (***largest group of freshwater lakes in the world***)

6. What are the names of the lakes found in the Great Lakes System? (***Lake Ontario, Lake Erie, Lake Huron, Lake Superior, Lake Michigan***)

7. Locate the Great Lakes on the map. Have the students identify each one.

8. Which lakes are shared by Canada and the United States? (***Ontario, Erie, Huron, Superior***)

9. Which Great Lake is entirely in the United States? (***Michigan***)

10. Into which river do the Great Lakes drain? (***St. Lawrence River***)

11. How was this inland waterway used years ago? (***It was the main route used by early explorers and settlers who lived in the United States and Canada.***)

12. Why did the areas around the St. Lawrence and the Great Lakes become highly industrialized? (***Transportation was cheap.***)

13. What did Canada and the United States begin to build in 1954? (***The St. Lawrence Seaway***)

14. Why was the seaway built? (***It was built to allow ocean-going vessels to travel further inland by going around rapids in the St. Lawrence River.***)

15. What else was built at the same time? (***hydro-electric power plants***)

16. Why did the people have to move from their homes and relocate somewhere else? (***The land was flooded and it became a reservoir called Lake St. Lawrence.***)

17. Which of the Great Lakes is the largest freshwater body in the world? (***Lake Superior***)

18. Which of the Great Lakes is the smallest? (***Lake Ontario***)

19. Which of the Great Lakes is the shallowest? (***Lake Erie***)

Follow-Ups:

1. Reproduce Map #8 entitled **"The Lakes of Canada"** (page 43). Discuss how lakes are shown on a map. Have the students look for the lakes found in each province. They should also take note of the ones found in their own province. Instruct the students to colour blue all the lakes that they find in Canada. The lakes found in their province may be circled green. Have them star any lake that they have seen or travelled on in their own province or territory and in the rest of Canada.

2. Reproduce Map #9 entitled **"The Great Lakes"** (page 44). Have the students locate each number on the map. On the line beside the number the students will neatly print the name of the lake, river or country. Below are the places the students are to label on the map:

1. Lake Superior	6. Detroit River	11. Ottawa
2. Lake Michigan	7. Lake Erie	12. Province of Ontario
3. Lake Huron	8. Niagara River	13. St. Mary's River
4. St. Clair River	9. Lake Ontario	14. The United States of America
5. Lake St. Clair	10. St. Lawrence River	

3. Reproduce Worksheets #10 (a) and (b) entitled **"Rivers and Lakes of Canada"** (pages 22 to 23). Divide your class into groups of four. Provide good Canadian atlases for the students to use to locate the rivers and lakes listed on the worksheet. Three students may peruse the maps while one records the answers on the worksheet or they all may search and record in a group.

Note: Information Sheets #4, 5 and 6 and the follow-up sheets #11, 12, 13, 14 and 15 may be discussed as well. Incorporate them as lessons if you so desire. They will provide students with the opportunity to read and interpret maps, graphs and charts.

Lessons #8 to #14

Expectations:

The students will:
• become familiar with the six regions of Canada.
• practise their reading and mapping skills.
• be aware of the interpendence of the provinces and territories

Discussion Time:

• Each region should be discussed independently and located on the map of Canada.
• Discuss the following topics for each area:

Location, Physical Surface, Climate, Waterways, Agriculture, Industries, Cities

Follow-ups:

• Complete all the fill in the blank worksheets and mapping activities for each area.
• The answers for the worksheets are found in the answer key.

WHERE IS CANADA?

Canada is the _____ largest country in the world. It covers the

_____ half of the continent called _____

except for Alaska. It shares this continent with the _____ and

_____. Canada is _____ sq. km in area.

_____ is larger than Canada.

What is a continent? _____

_____

What is an ocean? _____

_____

The seven continents found in the world are:

1. _____   5. _____

2. _____   6. _____

3. _____   7. _____

4. _____

The four oceans found in the world are:

1. _____   4. _____

2. _____   5. _____

3. _____

CANADA'S BORDERS

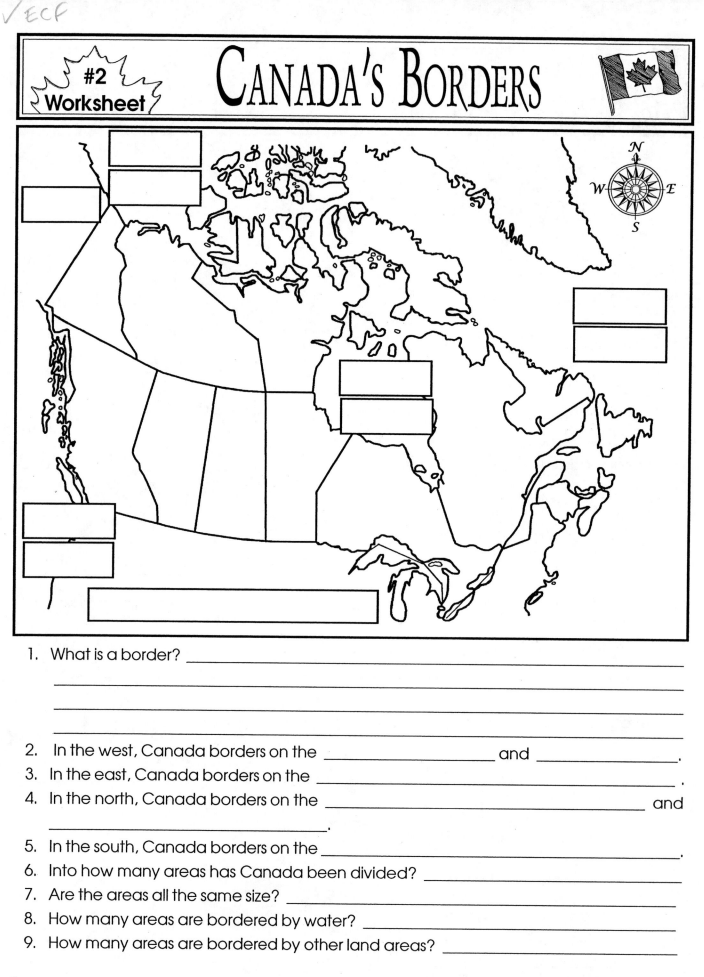

1. What is a border? _____
   _____
   _____
   _____

2. In the west, Canada borders on the _____ and _____.

3. In the east, Canada borders on the _____.

4. In the north, Canada borders on the _____ and
   _____.

5. In the south, Canada borders on the _____.

6. Into how many areas has Canada been divided? _____

7. Are the areas all the same size? _____

8. How many areas are bordered by water? _____

9. How many areas are bordered by other land areas? _____

1. Canada has _____ provinces and three _____.

2. The names of Canada's provinces and territories are listed on the flag. Can you write their names in the correct alphabetical order.

_____

_____

_____

_____

_____

_____

_____

_____

_____

_____

_____

_____

_____

Nunavut **Prince Edward Island**
Ontario **New Brunswick**
Alberta
Manitoba
Newfoundland & Labrador
Québec
Nova Scotia
Yukon Territory
Saskatchewan
British Columbia
Northwest Territories

3. Which province is an island? _____

4. Write the names of the Atlantic Provinces.

_____

_____

5. Write the names of the Prairie Provinces.

_____

6. Write the names of the territories.

_____

C/C

BORDER RIDDLES

Which Province or Territory Am I?

1. I border the Pacific Ocean on the west, Alberta on the east, the Yukon Territory and Northwest Territories on the north and the United States on the south.
   I am _____ .

2. I have a short land border on the north and a long border on the Atlantic Ocean.
   I am _____ .

3. I border the Great Lakes and the United States on the south, Québec on the east, Manitoba on the west and Hudson Bay on the north. I am _____ .

4. I border the Northwest Territories on the west, the Atlantic Ocean on the north and east, and Manitoba on the south. I am _____ .

5. I border Québec on the north, the United States on the west, the Atlantic Ocean on the east and the Bay of Fundy on the south. I am _____ .

6. My eastern border is on Nunavut, my northern border is the Arctic Ocean and my western border is on the Yukon Territory. I am _____ .

7. To the north I border the Northwest Territories, to the south I border the United States, on the east I border Saskatchewan and on the west I border British Columbia.
   I am _____ .

8. I border Nunavut on the north, the United States on the south, Ontario on the east and Saskatchewan on the west. I am _____ .

9. My western border is the state of Alaska, my eastern border is the Northwest Territories, my northern border is the Arctic Ocean and my southern border is British Columbia. I am _____ .

10. My border is the Atlantic Ocean. I am _____ .

11. I border Alberta on the west, Manitoba on the east, the Northwest Territories on the north and the United States on the south. I am _____ .

12. I border Ontario on the west, the United States and New Brunswick on the south, Newfoundland and Labrador on the east and James Bay, Hudson Bay and Ungava Bay on the north. I am _____ .

13. I border Québec on the west and south, and the Atlantic Ocean on the east as well, as all around me. I am _____ .

WORD SEARCH

Search for Each Province/Territory and its Capital City

In the Word Search look for the names of all the provinces and territories found in Canada . Circle each one green.
Look for the names of all the capital cities too. Circle each one red.

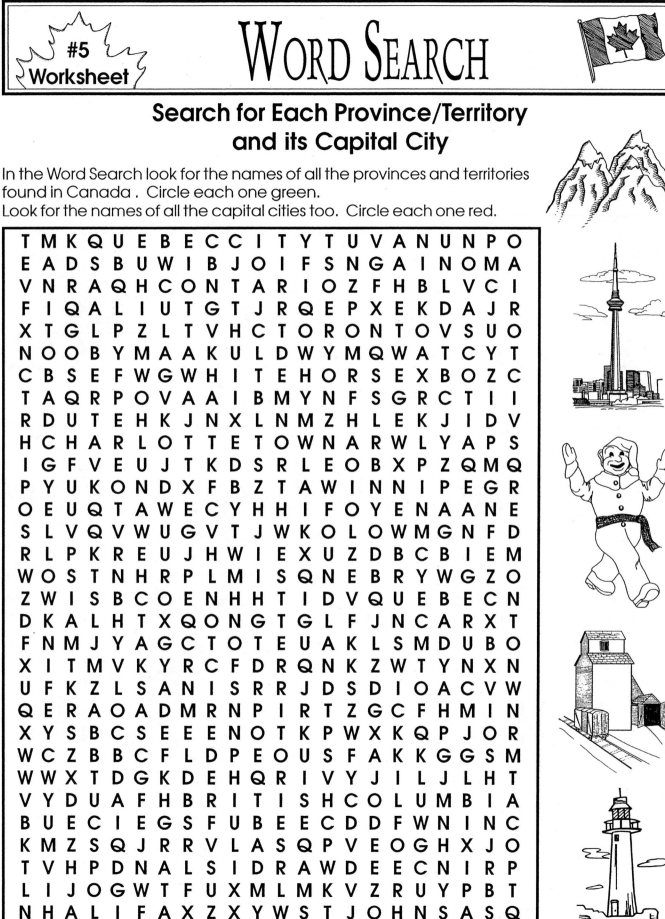

```
T M K Q U E B E C C I T Y T U V A N U N P O
E A D S B U W I B J O I F S N G A I N O M A
V N R A Q H C O N T A R I O Z F H B L V C I
F I Q A L I U T G T J R Q E P X E K D A J R
X T G L P Z L T V H C T O R O N T O V S U O
N O O B Y M A A K U L D W Y M Q W A T C Y T
C B S E F W G W H I T E H O R S E X B O Z C
T A Q R P O V A A I B M Y N F S G R C T I I
R D U T E H K J N X L N M Z H L E K J I D V
H C H A R L O T T E T O W N A R W L Y A P S
I G F V E U J T K D S R L E O B X P Z Q M Q
P Y U K O N D X F B Z T A W I N N I P E G R
O E U Q T A W E C Y H H I F O Y E N A A N E
S L V Q V W U G V T J W K O L O W M G N F D
R L P K R E U J H W I E X U Z D B C B I E M
W O S T N H R P L M I S Q N E B R Y W G Z O
Z W I S B C O E N H H T I D V Q U E B E C N
D K A L H T X Q O N G T G L F J N C A R X T
F N M J Y A G C T O T E U A K L S M D U B O
X I T M V K Y R C F D R Q N K Z W T Y N X N
U F K Z L S A N I S R R J D S D I O A C V W
Q E R A O A D M R N P I R T Z G C F H M I N
X Y S B C S E E E N O T K P W X K Q P J O R
W C Z B B C F L D P E O U S F A K K G G S M
W W X T D G K D E H Q R I V Y J I L J L H T
V Y D U A F H B R I T I S H C O L U M B I A
B U E C I E G S F U B E E C D D F W N I N C
K M Z S Q J R R V L A S Q P V E O G H X J O
T V H P D N A L S I D R A W D E E C N I R P
L I J O G W T F U X M L M K V Z R U Y P B T
N H A L I F A X Z X Y W S T J O H N S A S Q
```

#6 Worksheet — LET'S RESEARCH CANADA

1. Which territory in Canada is the largest? _____

2. Which province in Canada is the largest? _____

3. Which province is an island? _____

4. In which capital city will you find the largest shopping mall in Canada? _____

5. Which two capital cities are named after Queen Victoria? _____

6. In which provinces are the Rocky Mountains located? _____

7. Which capital city is known as "The Crossroads City"? _____

8. Which capital city has the largest population? _____

9. What is the floral emblem for Ontario? _____

10. Which territory has two very large lakes? _____

11. Which province has one of the Seven Wonders of the World? _____

12. Which capital city is the only walled city in North America outside Mexico?

_____

13. In which province will you find the flowerpot rocks? _____

14. In which province did the heroine of Lucy Maud Montgomery's classic story live?

_____

15. In which province would you find Peggy's Cove? _____

16. Which province has chosen the Puffin as its provincial bird? _____

17. In which capital city will you find Province House, the birthplace of Canada?

_____

18. Which capital city is located on the Saint John River? _____

19. Which island province is now connected to the mainland of Canada with a long

bridge? _____

20. In which province would you find totem poles? _____

Physical Regions of Canada

Physical Region: _____

Location	Land Forms	Minerals	Vegetation	Wildlife

Physical Region: _____

Location	Land Forms	Minerals	Vegetation	Wildlife

Physical Region: _____

Location	Land Forms	Minerals	Vegetation	Wildlife

1. Name three rivers that are tributaries of the St. Lawrence River.

   _____

   _____

2. Name four rivers that flow into James Bay.

   _____

   _____

3. Name four rivers that flow into Hudson Bay.

   _____

   _____

4. Which river has its source at Lake Ontario and its mouth at the Atlantic Ocean?

   _____

5. Name two rivers that flow into the Pacific Ocean.

   _____

6. Which two rivers flow through the three prairie provinces?

   _____

7. Name four rivers that flow north and empty into the Arctic Ocean.

   _____

   _____

8. Name the river whose name is the same as a territory.

   _____

9. On the map trace in blue all the rivers.

10. On the map circle in green the names of four rivers not entirely in Canada.

11. Underline in red the names of the rivers in your province or territory. Their names are:

   _____

   _____

   _____

   _____

HOW LONG ARE THE RIVERS OF CANADA?

There are many freshwater rivers in Canada. Each river is a different length. On the chart below arrange the names of Canada's Rivers from the largest to the smallest.

Canadian Rivers

Laird River 1 115
Fraser River 1 370
Yukon River 3 185
Athabasca River 1 231

St. Lawrence River 3 058
Churchill River 1 609
Mackenzie River 4 241

Ottawa River 1 271
Peace River 1 923
Columbia River 2 000

Name of River	Length in Kilometres	Flows Into
1.		
2.		
3.		
4.		
5.		
6.		
7.		
8.		
9.		
10.		

RIVERS AND LAKES OF CANADA

1. Using an atlas, locate the provinces and territories in which the following rivers are found.

   a) Saguenay River _____

   b) Trent River _____

   c) Madawaska River _____

   d) Abitibi River _____

   e) Peace River _____

   f) Fraser River _____

   g) Nelson River _____

   h) Saskatchewan River _____

   i) Detroit River _____

   j) St. Maurice River _____

   k) Ottawa River _____

   l) St. Clair River _____

   m) Slave River _____

   n) Skeena River _____

   o) Thames River _____

   p) Stikine River _____

   q) Qu'Appele River _____

   r) Thompson River _____

   s) Saint John River _____

   t) Gander River _____

2. Using an atlas locate the provinces and territories in which the following lakes are found. Classify each lake according to its province on the sheet provided.

Lake Louise	**Lake Simcoe**	**Lake Huron**	**Lake Winnipeg**
Lake Nipissing	**Great Slave Lake**	**Lake Nipigon**	**Lake of the Woods**
Lake Athabasca	**Great Bear Lake**	**Lake St. John**	**Lake Abitibi**
Lake St. Clair	**Lake Winnipegosis**	**Grand Lake**	**Lake Mistassini**
Lake Garry	**Smallwood Reservoir**	**Lake Aberdeen**	**Reindeer Lake**
Kootenay Lake	**Lake Okanagan**	**Lake Ontario**	**Lake Erie**

a) Newfoundland: _____

_____

b) Québec: _____

_____

c) Ontario: _____

_____

_____

_____

d) Manitoba: _____

_____

_____

e) Saskatchewan: _____

_____

f) Alberta: _____

_____

g) British Columbia: _____

_____

h) New Brunswick: _____

_____

i) Nunavut: _____

j) Northwest Territories: _____

_____

Canada is the _____ largest country in the world with nearly _____

_____ square kilometres of land. Its population is almost _____

_____ . About seventy-five percent of the people live within one hundred

and fifty kilometres of the southern border. Much of Canada is _____

because the country's terrain is _____ and its climate is quite

_____ in northern areas.

Listed below are the names of the provinces and territories and their populations. Complete the empty chart by listing the provinces and territories according to population from the smallest to the largest.

Province/Territory	Population	Province/Territory	Population
Newfoundland & Labrador	533 700	_____	_____
Prince Edward Island	138 500	_____	_____
New Brunswick	757 000	_____	_____
Nova Scotia	942 600	_____	_____
Québec	7 410 500	_____	_____
Ontario	11 874 400	_____	_____
Manitoba	1 150 000	_____	_____
Saskatchewan	1 015 700	_____	_____
Alberta	3 064 200	_____	_____
British Columbia	4 095 900	_____	_____
Yukon Territory	29 800	_____	_____
Northwest Territories	40 800	_____	_____
Nunavut	28 100	_____	_____

Using the facts on the chart that you have just organized, answer the following questions about Canada's population.

1. Star the province or territory in which you live and circle its population on the chart that you completed. What is the name of your province/territory and what is its population?

   _____

   Where does your province/territory rank with the other provinces/territories? _____

2. How does your province or territory rate in the size of its population?

   _____

3. Which province has the smallest population in Canada?

   _____

4. Which province is the most populated?

   _____

5. Which of the territories has the lowest population?

   _____

6. What is the total population of the Atlantic Provinces? _____

7. Which of the territories has the largest population?

   _____

8. Which of the Atlantic Provinces has the highest population?

   _____

9. Which of the Prairie provinces has the smallest population?

   _____

10. What is the total population of the Prairie Provinces? _____

11. What is the difference between Ontario's and Québec's population? _____

12. How many more people live in Newfoundland and Labrador than in Prince Edward Island?

    _____

13. Does the total population of the three territories equal the population of Prince Edward Island? _____ Which area has the larger population?

    _____

ETHNIC POPULATION OF CANADA

Canada's population is made up of many cultures and people. These immigrants and their descendents came from various countries around the world.

Look at the population circle graph to find out who lives in Canada.

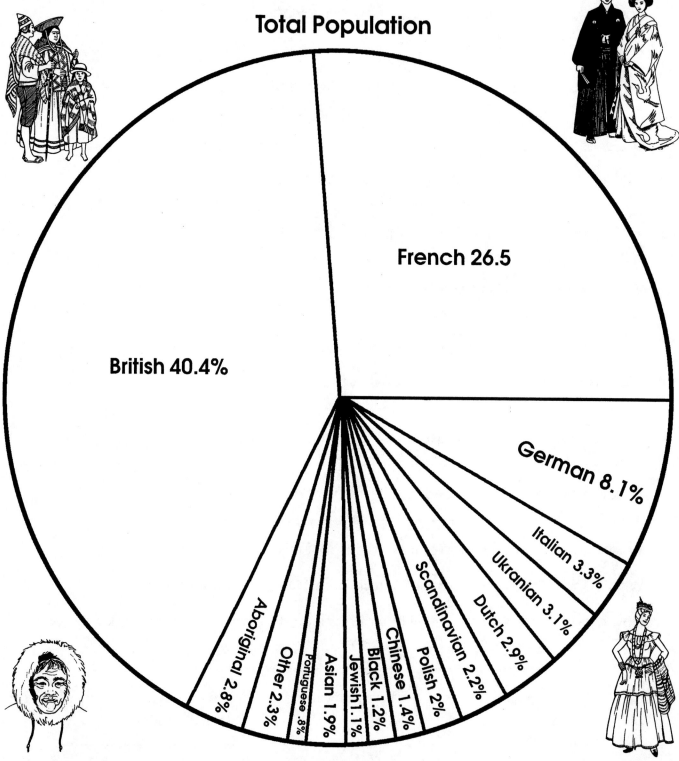

Total Population

British 40.4%

French 26.5

German 8.1%

Italian 3.3%

Ukranian 3.1%

Dutch 2.9%

Scandinavian 2.2%

Polish 2%

Chinese 1.4%

Black 1.2%

Jewish 1.1%

Asian 1.9%

Portuguese .8%

Other 2.3%

Aboriginal 2.8%

SSJ1-38

ETHNIC POPULATION OF CANADA

Use the circle graph to locate the answers to the following questions.

1. Of what descent are most of the people in Canada? _____

2. Are there more aboriginal people than Chinese living in Canada? _____

3. What are the three largest ethnic groups found in Canada? _____
   _____

4. What are the three smallest ethnic groups? _____
   _____

5. Are there more Dutch people than Ukrainian people in Canada? _____

Ethnic Populations

Rank the ethnic populations from 1 to 15 going from the largest to the smallest

Aboriginal: 700 616 _____

East and Southeast Asian: 499 439 _____

Black: 300 264 _____

British 10 133 914 _____

Chinese: 350 308 _____

Dutch: 725 638 _____

French: 6 655 854 _____

German: 2 026 782 _____

Italian: 825 726 _____

Jewish: 277 421 _____

Other: 575 506 _____

Polish: 500 440 _____

Portuguese: 200 176 _____

Scandinavian: 550 484 _____

Ukrainian: 775 682 _____

The ethnic group with the largest population is _____ .

The ethnic group with the smallest population is _____ .

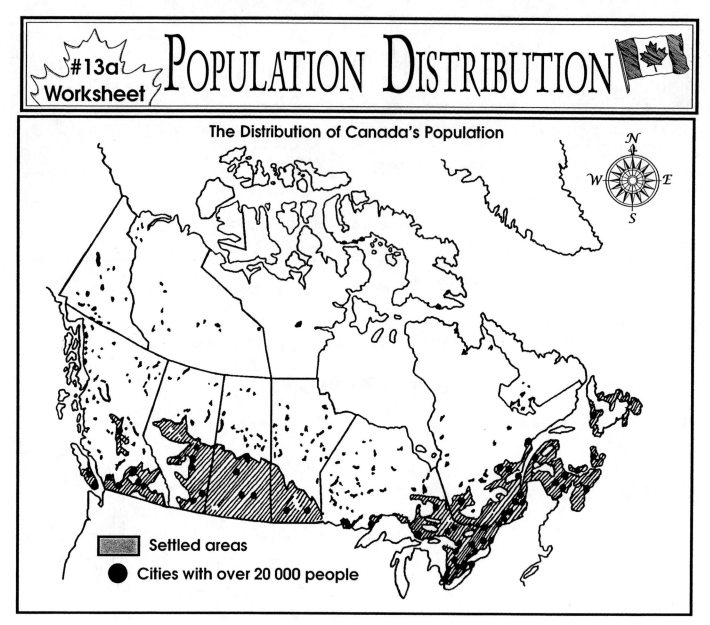

The Distribution of Canada's Population

Settled areas

● Cities with over 20 000 people

1. Examine the population map of Canada carefully.

2. Where do most of the people in Canada live?

   _____

   _____

3. In which three provinces do you find the most cities over 20 000 people?

   _____

   _____

4. Why do you think most of the people live in these areas?

   _____

   _____

5. In which areas do very few people live?

   _____

   _____

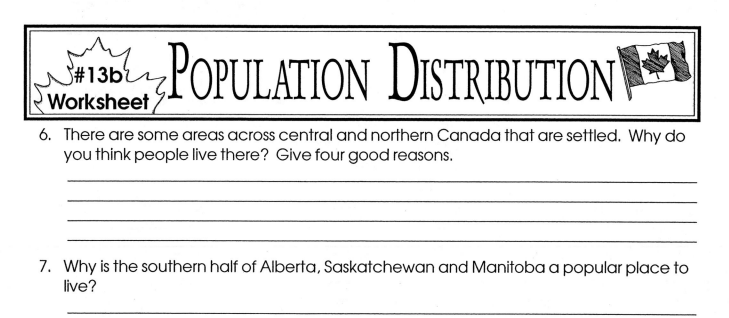

6. There are some areas across central and northern Canada that are settled. Why do you think people live there? Give four good reasons.

_____

_____

_____

_____

7. Why is the southern half of Alberta, Saskatchewan and Manitoba a popular place to live?

_____

_____

_____

8. Why do the areas close to the Great Lakes have so many large cities?

_____

_____

_____

_____

9. Why are the three territories so sparsely populated?

_____

_____

_____

_____

10. Describe the density of the population in the area in which you live? List the ethnic backgrounds that make up the area.

_____

_____

_____

_____

_____

11. Eventually some areas will become over-populated. What do you think the government should do to prevent over-population?

_____

_____

_____

_____

_____

_____

#14a Worksheet CLIMATIC REGIONS OF CANADA

Which region is it?

Southeastern Region	**Prairie Region**	**Pacific Region**
Northern Region	**Arctic Region**	**Mountain Region**

1. Its winters are mild and its temperatures seldom go below freezing.

   _____

2. Its winters last eight to ten months and are extremely cold.

   _____

3. The winters are cold and last up to six months. Summers are short and cool.

   _____

4. This region has very cold winters with hot, dry summers.

   _____

5. Valleys are warmer than the mountains and northern areas.

   _____

6. Winters are cold in one area and mild in another.

   _____

Let's Compare Temperatures!

Look at the **Climatic Map of Canada**. Locate the different temperatures of the cities that are labelled. Answer the following questions.

1. Is Prince Rupert, British Columbia colder than Moosonee, Ontario in the winter? _____
2. How much colder is Ottawa in the winter than Niagara Falls. _____
3. What is the temperature of Victoria, British Columbia in the summer? _____
4. What is the difference in temperature between Iqaluit and Halifax in the winter? _____
5. Which place in Canada has the coldest summer and winter? _____
6. Why do you think Prince George is colder in the winter than Prince Rupert and Kamloops?

   _____

   _____

7. Which city is -29° C in the winter and 15° C in the summer?

   _____

8. Which two places have the same temperature in the summer?

   _____

Climatic Map of Canada

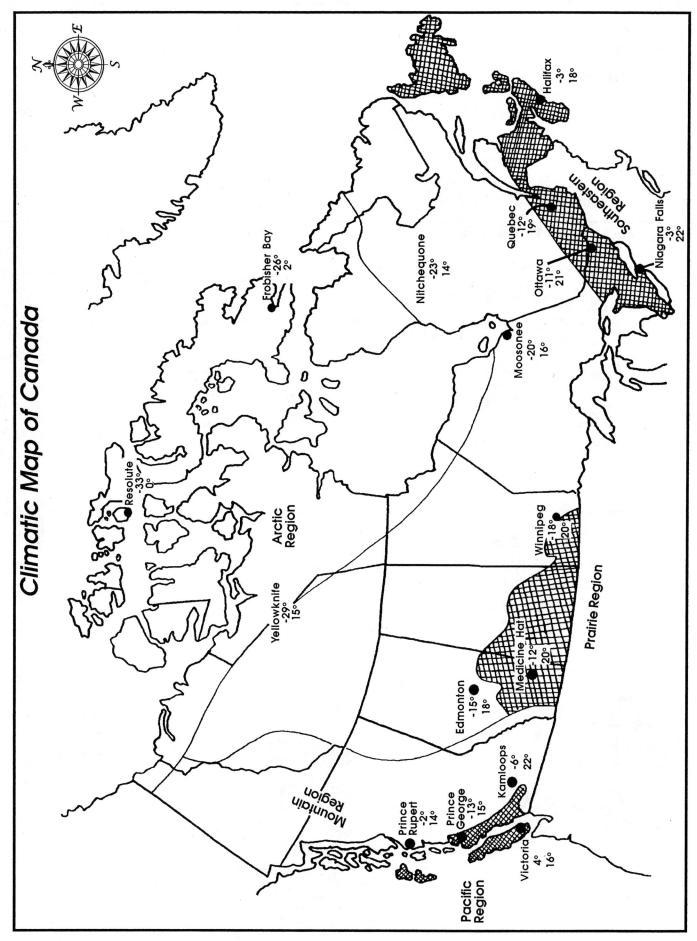

Resolute
-33°
0°

Frobisher Bay
-26°
2°

Yellowknife
-29°
15°

Arctic Region

Nitchequone
-23°
14°

Quebec
-12°
19°

Halifax
-3°
18°

Southeastern Region

Ottawa
-11°
21°

Niagara Falls
-3°
22°

Moosonee
-20°
16°

Winnipeg
-18°
20°

Prairie Region

Medicine Hat
-12°
20°

Edmonton
-15°
18°

Mountain Region

Kamloops
-6°
22°

Prince Rupert
-2°
14°

Prince George
-13°
15°

Victoria
4°
16°

Pacific Region

SSJ1-38

PRECIPITATION AND TEMPERATURE

The bar graph below shows the precipitation and temperature ranges for most of the capital cities of Canada.

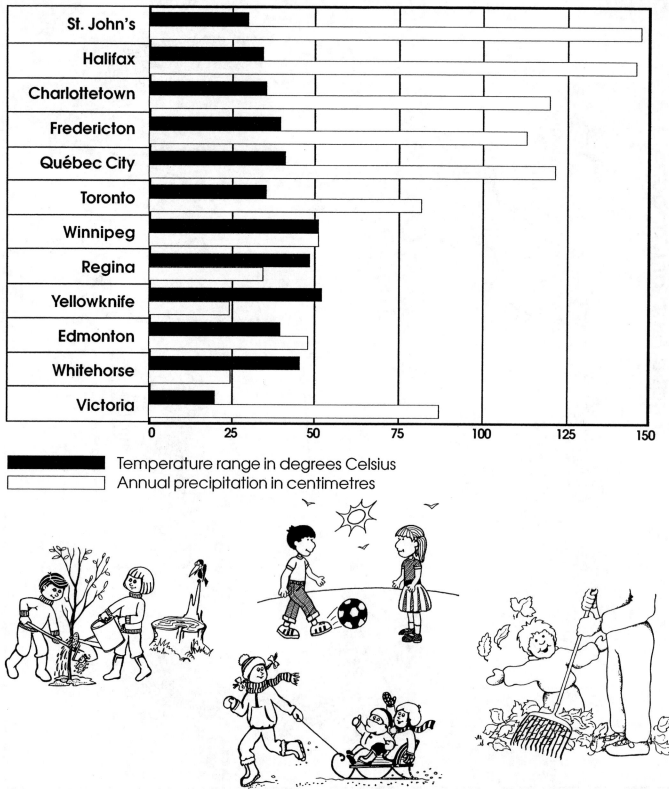

Temperature range in degrees Celsius
Annual precipitation in centimetres

SSJ1-38

PRECIPITATION AND TEMPERATURE

Examine the graph carefully then answer the following questions.

1. Which capital city only received 50 centimetres of rain? _____

2. Which capital city has the highest temperature range? _____

3. Which capital city had the lowest range in temperature? _____

4. Which capital city receives the most rainfall? _____

5. Which city has the same range in temperature and annual rainfall? _____

6. Which two cities receive more than 125 centimetres of rainfall each year?

    _____

7. How many cities receive more than 75 centimetres of rainfall each year? _____

    _____

    _____

8. Which cities receive less than 25 centimetres of rain each year?

    _____

Community Climate

Find out the following things about your local community:

1. What is the average temperature in your community during the summer? _____

2. What is the average temperature in your community during the winter? _____

3. What is the average temperature in your community during the spring? _____

4. What is the average temperature in your community during autumn? _____

5. How many centimetres of rainfall does your community receive in a year? _____

6. How many centimetres of snowfall does your community receive in a year? _____

7. What is the highest temperature that your community has ever experienced during a

    summer? _____

8. What is the coldest temperature that your community has ever experienced during a

    winter? _____

Natural Vegetation Regions of Canada

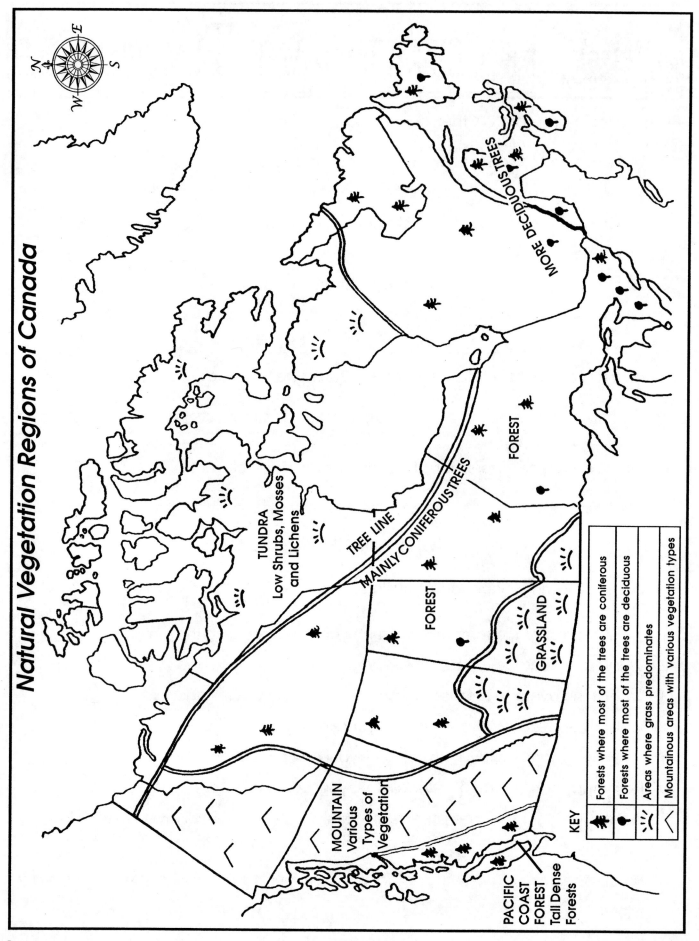

MORE DECIDUOUS TREES

FOREST

TREE LINE

MAINLY CONIFEROUS TREES

TUNDRA
Low Shrubs, Mosses
and Lichens

FOREST

GRASSLAND

MOUNTAIN
Various
Types of
Vegetation

PACIFIC
COAST
FOREST
Tall Dense
Forests

KEY

	Forests where most of the trees are coniferous
	Forests where most of the trees are deciduous
	Areas where grass predominates
	Mountainous areas with various vegetation types

34

SSJ1-38

NATURAL VEGETATION REGIONS

Throughout Canada different types of vegetation are able to grow. Canada's varied climate affects the type of vegetation found in certain areas.

Examine the map entitled **"Natural Vegetation Regions of Canada"**.

Locate the answers to the following questions.

1. What types of trees grow in Newfoundland? _____

2. What types of vegetation grow above the treeline?
    _____

3. In which province are the trees tall and the forests dense? _____

4. Which provinces have grasslands?
    _____

5. In which territories and provinces would you find tundra?
    _____
    _____

6. In which provinces would you find deciduous trees growing?
    _____
    _____

7. Which provinces and territory have a variety of things growing in the mountains?
    _____
    _____

8. What is a coniferous tree? _____
    _____
    _____

    Name three coniferous trees that grow in Canada. _____
    _____

9. What is a deciduous tree? _____
    _____
    _____

    Name three deciduous trees that grow in Canada. _____
    _____

10. What is tundra? _____
    _____

Map #1

Map of the World: Where is Canada?

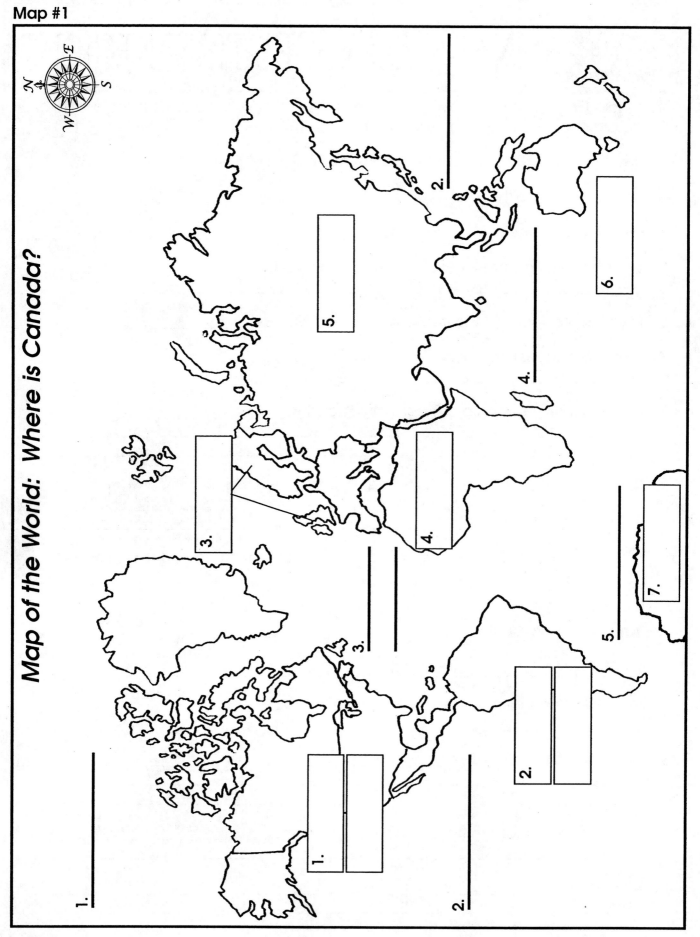

36

Map #2

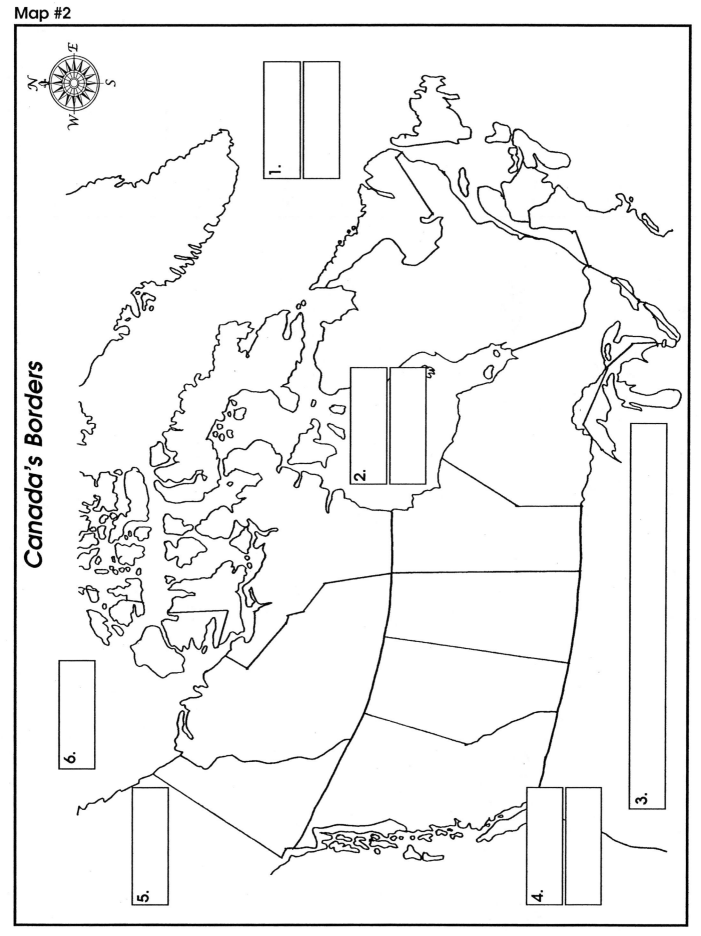

Canada's Borders

1.

2.

3.

4.

5.

6.

Map #3

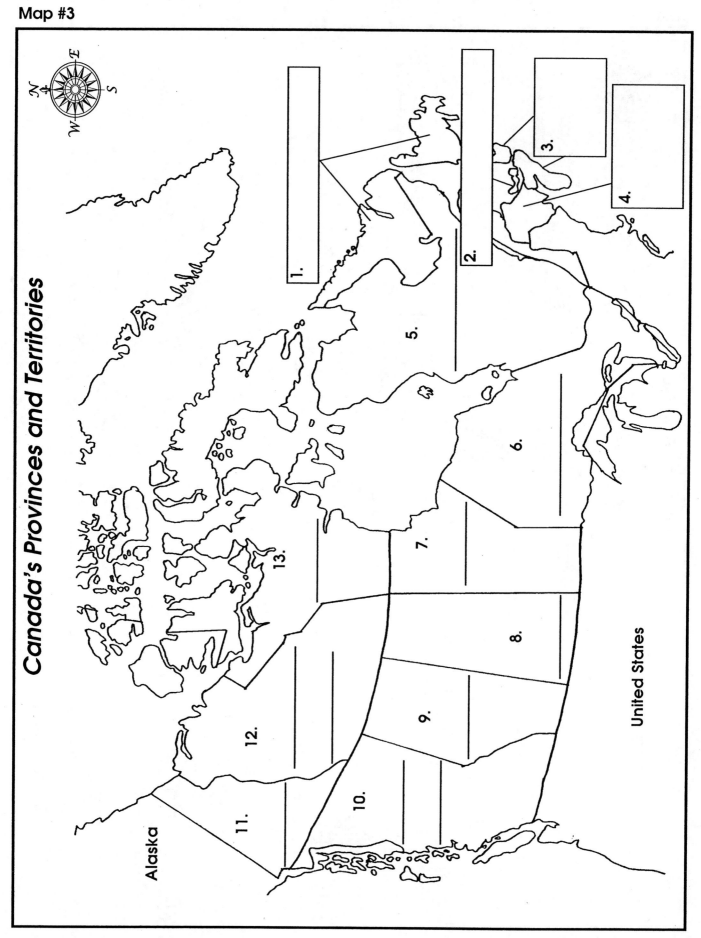

Canada's Provinces and Territories

1.

2.

3.

4.

5.

6.

7.

8.

9.

10.

11.

12.

13.

Alaska

United States

38

Map #4

Borders Inside Canada

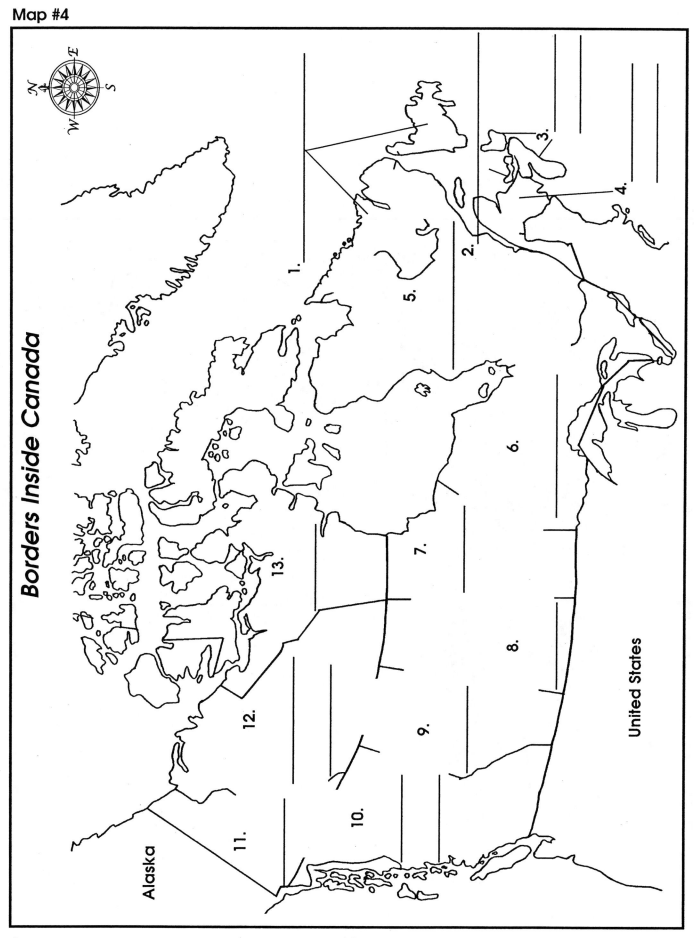

Alaska

United States

Map #5

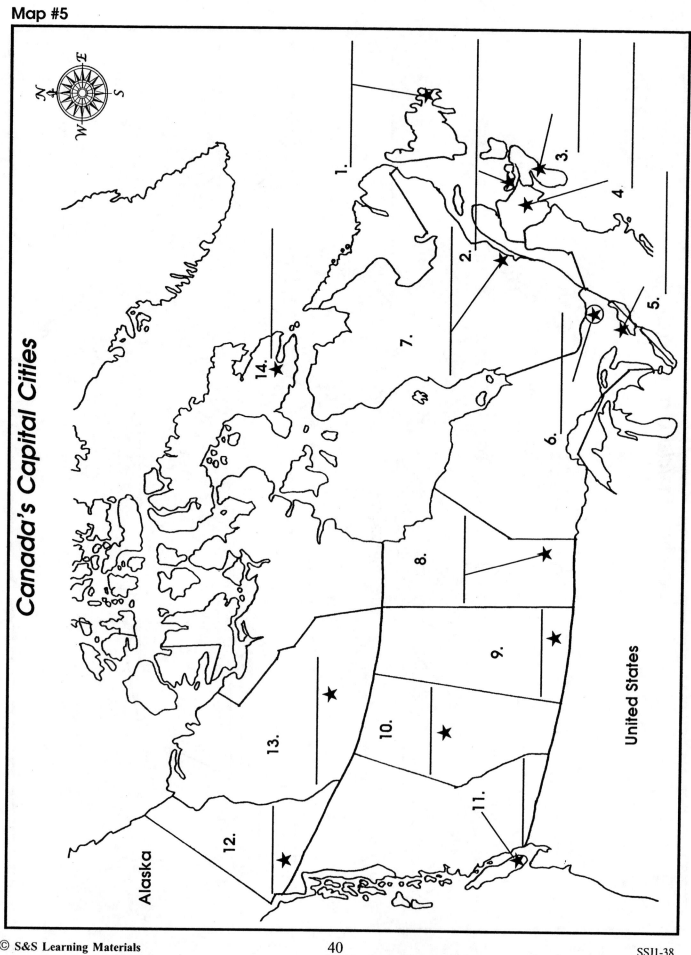

Map #5 — Canada's Capital Cities

Map #6

The Physical Regions of Canada

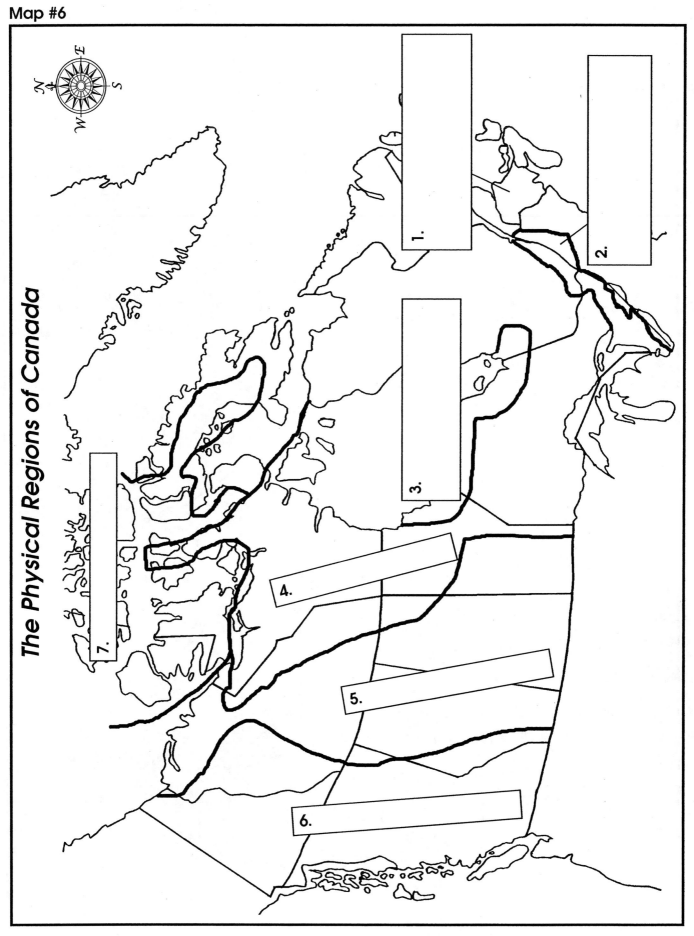

1.

2.

3.

4.

5.

6.

7.

Map #7

The Rivers of Canada

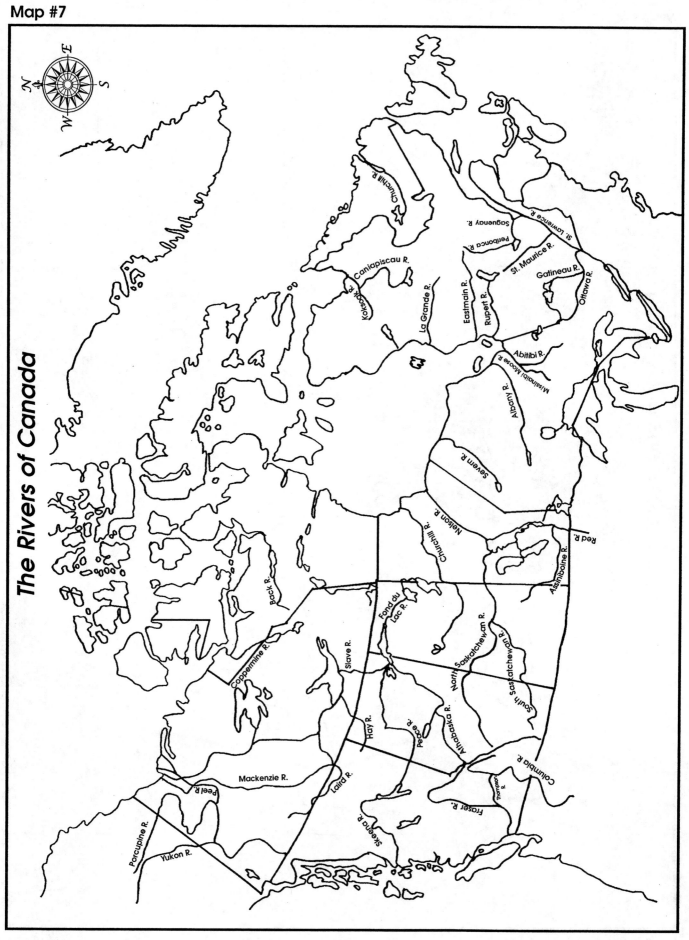

Map #8

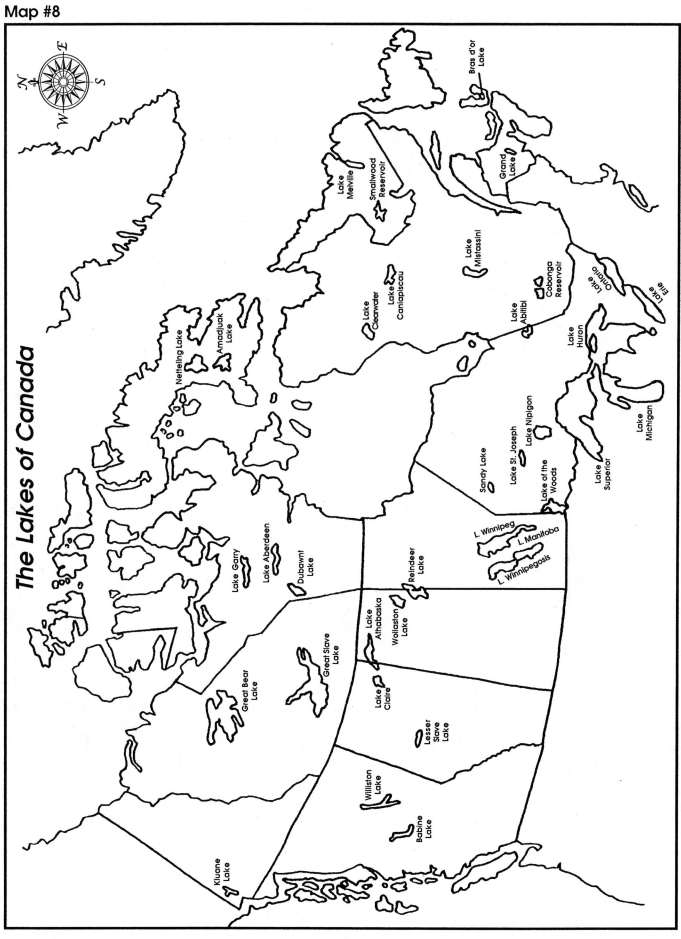

The Lakes of Canada

Map #9

The Great Lakes

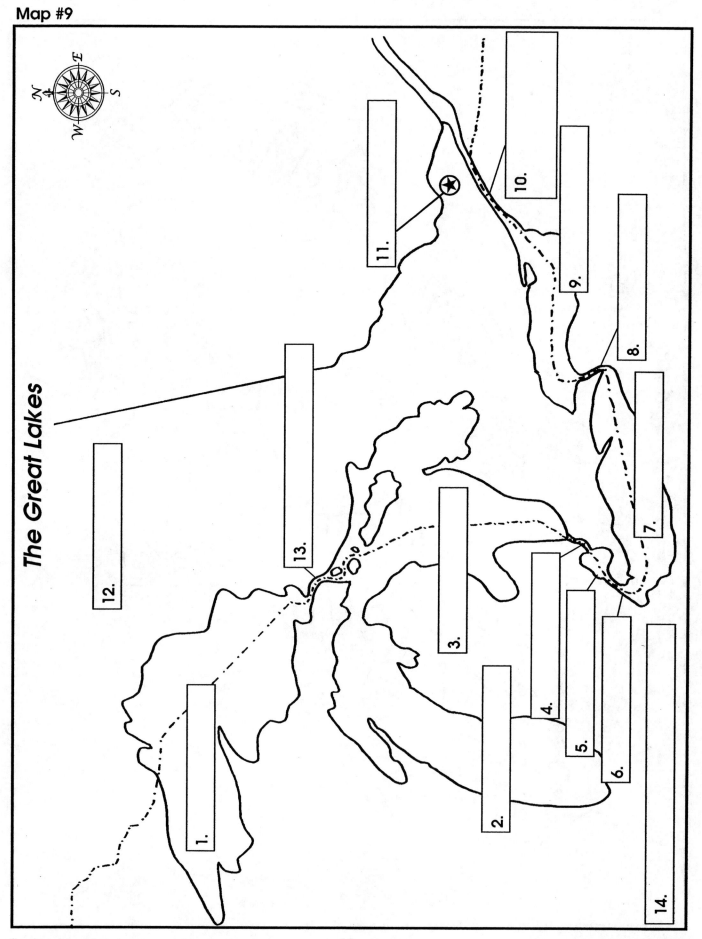

The Physical Regions of Canada

Canada has seven major land regions. They are:

1. The Cordillera Region
2. The Arctic Lowlands
3. The Interior Plains or Lowlands
4. The Canadian Shield
5. The Hudson Bay Lowlands
6. The St. Lawrence Lowlands
7. The Appalachian Region

The Cordillera Region

The Cordillera Region consists of the Pacific Coastal Mountain Ranges and Lowlands and the Rocky Mountains. Both of these regions consist of a very large group of mountains that extend from Alaska through to Mexico.

The Pacific Coastal Mountain Ranges and Lowlands

The Pacific Coastal Mountain Ranges and Lowlands are found in British Columbia and the southwestern part of the Yukon Territory. This region occupies almost all of British Columbia. The Queen Charlotte Islands and Vancouver Island are also included in this region. These islands are the top part of a mountain range that is partly covered by the Pacific Ocean. The Coast Mountains and St. Elias Mountains are found in this region also. Canada's highest mountain, Mount Logan, is found in the St. Elias Mountains in the Yukon near the Alaskan border. It stands 5 951 metres above sea level. Glaciers cover many of the mountains found in the St. Elias Range.

The Coast Mountains run close to the coastline of British Columbia and have made many inlets called fiords. The fiords are long and narrow inlets that provide water routes to many valuable forests. These dense forests contain tall red cedars, hemlocks and other evergreen trees that grow on the lower slopes of the mountains. Many fur-bearing animals such as black bears and foxes make their homes in the forested areas.

East of the Coast Mountains lies an interior plateau that consists of valleys, plains and small mountains. Many mineral resources such as bismuth and molybdenum have made this area very valuable. Farms, orchards and grasslands for grazing cattle are found on the southern part of the interior plateau.

The Rocky Mountains

The Rocky Mountains are located to the east of the Pacific Ranges and Lowlands.

Mountains in the Rockies are often snow-capped and vary in height from 2 100 metres to 3 660 metres above sea level. Mount Robson is the tallest peak in eastern British Columbia and stands 3 954 metres high.

PHYSICAL REGIONS OF CANADA

The Rocky Mountain Chain is 4 800 kilometres long and extends from New Mexico to Alaska. The Canadian Rockies stretch from Canada's southern border to the Laird River in British Columbia. The Selwyn Mountains and the Mackenzie Mountains are found between the Laird River and the Alaskan border. In southern British Columbia, the Columbia Mountains are separated from the Canadian Rockies by a long, narrow valley called the Rocky Mountain Trench.

Rich deposits of coal, lead, silver, zinc and other minerals are found in the Rocky Mountains. Large forests of juniper and pine trees grow on the Rockies' lower slopes. Firs and spruces are able to survive at higher elevations. Animals such as bears, deer, minks, mountain lions, squirrels and many others live in the forests on the upper slopes. Above the timber line, an area where trees cannot grow, Rocky Mountain Goats and Bighorn Sheep roam. Many types of fish inhabit the swift-flowing mountain streams.

The Arctic Lowlands

The Arctic Lowlands are found within the Arctic Circle. The Arctic Lowlands consist of twelve large islands and hundreds of smaller ones. Most of the islands are barren and unexplored. Baffin Island and Ellesmere Island, which are two of the largest islands, have many glaciers, tall mountains and fiords. Victoria Island is very flat. The seas around these many islands are frozen most of the year.

The Arctic Lowlands consist of tundras which are areas too cold and dry for trees to grow. The subsoil is permanently frozen and only a thin layer thaws during the short, cool summers. Simple plants such as lichens, mosses, grasses and sedges grow in the lowlands. Caribou and musk oxen graze on the tundras. Other wildlife that make their homes in this region are Arctic foxes, Arctic hares, lemmings, polar bears, ptarmigans, seals, walruses and whales. During the summer, insects thrive on the islands.

Petroleum and natural gas, lead and zinc have been discovered in some of the western Arctic Islands but none of it has been taken out due to high production and transportation costs.

The Interior Plains

The Interior Plains are located in the northeastern corner of British Columbia, most of Alberta and Saskatchewan, and the southwestern part of Manitoba. This region extends north through the Northwest Territories to the Arctic Ocean.

The Interior Plains are covered in prairie grasslands in the south. The soil is rich and black and farmers grow wheat and other grains in it. In southern Alberta, the grasslands are used by ranchers for their cattle to graze on. The northern areas of the Interior Plains are heavily forested with white spruce and jack pines. Deer, elk, moose and

other fur-bearing animals inhabit the forested areas. Near the Arctic Ocean the land becomes tundra covered by snow for more than half the year.

The Interior Plains are rich with many mineral deposits. Alberta has become a major mining area due to its large deposits of petroleum, natural gas and coal. One of the world's largest tar sands (sands that contain oil) lies along the Athabaska River in Alberta. Important deposits of petroleum, uranium and potash are found in southern Saskatchewan. In the Northwest Territories petroleum, lead and zinc have been found.

The Canadian Shield

The Canadian Shield is a huge horseshoe-shaped region that curves around Hudson Bay from the Arctic Coast of the Northwest Territories to the coast of Labrador and the mainland of Newfoundland. It covers about one half of Canada and is made up of very old rock.

Thousands of lakes and rivers and many low hills are found in the Canadian Shield. The many rivers break into rapids and waterfalls at the edge of the region. Hydro-electric plants have been built on many rivers and supply hydro-electric power to many factories and homes in cities and towns in Québec, Ontario and Manitoba.

Very few people live in the northern part of the Canadian Shield as the soil is poor and the climate is quite cold. Some northern areas of the Canadian Shield are tundras and the plants and animals that live there are the same as the ones found in the Arctic Lowlands. The Canadian Shield is heavily forested in many northern areas. Deer, elk, moose, wolves and smaller animals live in the forests.

The southern edge of the Canadian Shield does have soil that is good for farming. It is close to large cities such as Ottawa, Toronto and Montreal. The many lakes and ski slopes in this area are used by the people who live in these cities.

A great deal of Canada's mineral wealth is located in the Canadian Shield. Iron ore comes from mines in Québec. Cobalt, copper, gold, nickel and uranium are mined near Sudbury, Ontario. The Canadian Shield also contains minerals such as platinum, silver and zinc.

The Hudson Bay Lowlands

The Hudson Bay Lowlands are a flat, swampy region between the Canadian Shield and the southwestern coast of Hudson Bay. The Lowlands are covered with poor-quality forests and large deposits of peat, a decayed vegetable matter. There are very few settled areas in the lowlands. The only permanent settlements are small villages, trading posts and ports such as Churchill and Moosonee.

The St. Lawrence Lowlands

The St. Lawrence Lowlands is the smallest land region in Canada. More than half the people in Canada live in this region. The St. Lawrence Lowlands is made up of flat and rolling countryside along the St. Lawrence River and the Peninsula of Southern Ontario. It also includes the Island of Anticosti found at the mouth of the St. Lawrence River which is a wilderness because it is isolated and has a colder climate.

Canada's major deciduous forests are located in Southern Ontario. These trees shed their leaves every fall. The forests are filled with beech, hickory, maple, oak and walnut trees. Many small animals such as squirrels, rabbits, raccoons and porcupines inhabit the forested areas.

The St. Lawrence Lowlands is the major manufacturing centre of Canada because it has excellent transportation facilities and lies near markets in the eastern and central United States. Fertile soil and a mild climate allow farmers to grow many varieties of fruits and vegetables. Many dairy farms are located in this region.

The Appalachian Region

The Appalachian Region includes southeastern Québec and all of the Atlantic Provinces. The Appalachian Mountains are an ancient chain that extends from the island of Newfoundland and Labrador south to the state of Alabama in the United States. The land in this region is generally hilly. Many of the mountains have been worn down by glaciers and erosion. The highest mountains are the Shickshock Mountains found in the Gaspé Peninsula in Québec.

Most of the people who live in the Appalachian Region make their homes along the coast. Hundreds of bays and inlets provide excellent harbours for fishing boats. Parts of Newfoundland and Labrador and Nova Scotia have steep, rocky coastlines.

Evergreen trees and deciduous trees grow in the many forests found in the region. Good farmland is found in Prince Edward Island, along the St. John River in New Brunswick and in the Annapolis River in Nova Scotia. Québec has the world's richest deposits of asbestos. Coal and gypsum are mined in New Brunswick. Copper, lead and zinc are mined in Newfoundland and Labrador and New Brunswick.

SSJ1-38

A "river" is a large body of water that moves over the land in a long channel. The "source" of a river usually begins high up in mountains or hills. The river's water comes from a combination of rainfall, lakes, springs and melting ice and snow. Small streams flow from the river's source. These streams are called its "headwaters". The headwaters flow into tiny, narrow channels called "rills". As the rills move downhill, they come together to form wider and deeper channels called "brooks" The brooks then join together to make "streams" and the streams join to form "rivers". All the rills, brooks and streams that carry water to a river are called "tributaries". The river and its tributaries form a "river system". Some river systems have several small rivers that flow into larger ones.

Parts of a River System

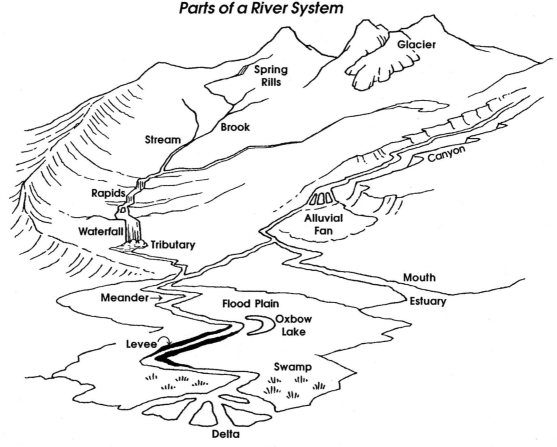

A river receives most of its water from rainfall. The rain flows over the land into the waters of the river system. The water eventually reaches the largest river in the system by way of rills, brooks, streams and smaller rivers. The rain also soaks into the ground and gathers as ground water. The ground water seeps into the river system and keeps the water flowing in most rivers during dry periods.

The waters of a river system drain an area of land. This is called the system's "drainage basin". North America is split into two large drainage basins by an imaginary line called the "Continental Divide". Water from the eastern side of the divide flows toward the Atlantic Ocean, Arctic Ocean or Gulf of Mexico. Water from the western side of the divide flows toward the Pacific Ocean.

WHAT IS A RIVER?

The "channel" of a river consists of the land on either side of and beneath the flowing water. The bottom of the channel is the "bed" and the edges are the river "banks". The channel slopes steeply near the "source" of the river and almost flat at the "mouth". The flow of water of most rivers is faster in the middle course. The "mouth" of a river is where the river empties its waters into another body of water such as a lake, ocean or larger river. The flow of the river's water slows down dramatically at the river's mouth. Sometimes this decrease in speed causes a body of land called a "delta" to form. Deltas are made of rock and dirt carried by the river; the rock and dirt settle where the river slows down. This material is called the river's "load".

"Waterfalls" and "rapids" are found in a river. A waterfall occurs when the river crosses a layer of strong resistant rock. Downstream the rock has been worn away by the river's flow which leaves a steep drop in the river's channel. The water passes over the edge of the harder layer and falls to the lower part of the channel.

Rapids occur when water tumbles over large boulders or rock ledges in the river channel. Fast flowing rivers sometimes cut a canyon, a deep channel with high walls worn into the river's bed. A river's flow may also cut valleys through the land. The force of the river erodes the land to create a steep, "v-shaped valley" that rises from the river's banks. A flat area may occur on one or both sides of the banks of a river. This area is called the "flood plain" and is covered by river water during floods.

Some rivers have flood plains hundreds of kilometres wide. In a flood plain the river channel tends to curve from one side of the plain to another. These snake-like bends are called "meanders".

There are many large rivers found in Canada. They are:

Athabasca River	Nelson River	Saint Mary's River
Churchill River	Niagara River	Saskatchewan River
Columbia River	Ottawa River	Skeena River
Detroit River	Peace River	Winnipeg River
Fraser River	Red River of the North	Yukon River
Mackenzie River	Restigouche River	Richelieu River
Miramichi River	Saguenay River	Saint John River
St. Lawrence River		

The Mackenzie River is the longest river in Canada and its length is 1 724 kilometres. The St. Lawrence River is the second longest measuring 1 300 kilometres.

WHAT IS A RIVER?

A lake is a body of water surrounded by land. The word *lake* comes from a Greek word which means "hole" or "pond". Most lakes were formed by glaciers. In the mountains, lakes were formed when glaciers carved deep valleys as they travelled. The basins they carved then filled up with water to form lakes. In other regions, glaciers gouged hollows in the land and deposited rocks and earth as they melted.

Lakes are fed by rivers and mountain streams. Some are fed by underground springs or streams. Some lakes have water running in, but none running out.

Lakes provide trade and travel routes and water for farmers to use to irrigate their fields. They supply water to communities and are used to generate electric power. People also use them for recreational purposes.

The Great Lakes are the world's largest group of freshwater lakes. They are Lake Superior, Lake Michigan, Lake Huron, Lake Erie and Lake Ontario. The Great Lakes form the most important inland waterway in North America. They were the main route used by early explorers and settlers who located in Canada and the United States. The areas along the Great Lakes and the St. Lawrence River became great industrial centres in Canada and the United States because transportation was cheap.

Four of the Great Lakes are shared by Canada and the United States and they form a boundary between the two countries. Lake Michigan lies entirely in the United States. The Great Lakes drain into the St. Lawrence River.

Rapids on the St. Lawrence prevented large ocean vessels from travelling to ports on the Great Lakes. In 1954, Canada and the United States began to build the St. Lawrence Seaway. This project took five years to build. The Seaway was to become a major commercial waterway that would link the Atlantic Ocean and the Great Lakes. The Seaway was formed by the St. Lawrence River, several lakes and a system of canals and locks. This waterway enables ocean-going vessels to travel further inland to ports located in Canada and the United States.

Power stations were also built to produce hydro-electric power to be used by both countries. Railways, highways, six villages and towns, and people had to be relocated as 16 000 hectares of land was going to be flooded in Ontario and New York State to create a new reservoir called Lake St. Lawrence. The reservoir would hold water to be used to make hydro-electric power. New communities were created near the reservoir.

In Canada you will find the following large freshwater lakes.

Lake Athabasca	Reindeer Lake	Lake Saint Clair
Lake Erie	Great Slave Lake	Lake Superior
Lake Huron	Lake Nipigon	Lake Winnipegosis
Lake Louise	Great Bear Lake	Lake Manitoba
Lake of the Woods	Smallwood Reservoir	Lake Winnipeg
Lake Ontario	Lesser Slave Lake	

THE POPULATION OF CANADA

There are approximately thirty million people who live in Canada. Canada is the second largest country in the world and has an area of ten million square kilometres. There is an average of three people per square kilometre. Compare that to the United States where there are twenty-eight people per square kilometre and Japan where there are 335 people per square kilometre.

Since World War Two, Canada's population has doubled. Almost all Canadians are of European descent. The First Nations People and the Inuit make up about two percent of the nation's population. The Inuit live mainly in the northern areas of the Northwest Territories, Newfoundland and Labrador, Ontario and Nunavut.

The First Nations People belong to one of ten major groups such as the Algonquian, the Athapaskan, the Haida, the Iroquoian, the Kootenayan, the Salishan, the Siouan, the Tlingit, the Tsimshian and the Wakashan. The majority of the First Nations People live on reserves or reservations across Canada.

Early immigrants came from Britain, Germany, Greece, Italy, the Netherlands, Portugal and Latin America. Many Canadians are refugees from other countries who were involved in revolutions. These people came from Hungary, Cambodia, Laos and Vietnam. Since Hong Kong was given back to China by the British, many Chinese immigrants have come to Canada and live in the Toronto area and in British Columbia. The Prairie Provinces were settled mainly by Ukrainians and Germans. Many black immigrants of West Indian descent who came from French and English speaking islands such as Haiti and Trinidad have made their homes in Canada as well.

In Canada, two official languages are spoken. They are English and French. French is mainly spoken in Québec while English is mainly used in the rest of the country. Other languages are often spoken in the homes of different nationalities in order to maintain and preserve the language.

52

Canada's climate changes as you travel from east to west, and even from south to north.

In the Mountain Region on the western coast of Canada, the winter and summer conditions vary greatly in different parts of the region. Valleys and southern areas are generally warmer than in the mountains and northern areas. Precipitation is also varied. The Western slopes of the mountains usually receive more precipitation than the eastern slopes.

In the Pacific Region the winters are mild with temperatures above freezing. Summers are warm. Precipitation is quite heavy and comes mainly in the winter.

The Prairie Region has very cold winters and hot, dry summers. Precipitation is light and comes mainly in the summer.

The Arctic Region has extremely cold winters which last eight to ten months. Precipitation is very slight.

The Northern Region of Canada has cold winters that last up to six months. Summers are cool and short. Precipitation is moderate and occurs mainly in the summer.

The Southeastern Region has cold winters in the central area and milder ones in the southwest area. Summers are usually warm. A moderate amount of rainfall is experienced.

Climatic Regions of Canada

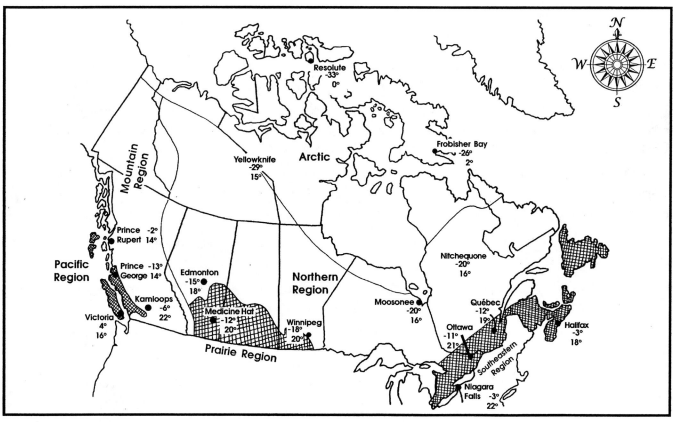

CANADA'S NATURAL VEGETATION

Forest, grassland and tundra are the major vegetation zones in Canada. There are fourteen different vegetation zones altogether. They are:

Arctic Tundra	Subarctic or Transition Forest Region
Taiga or Boreal Forest Region	Mixed Woods
Parkland	Prairie
Great Lakes -St. Lawrence Forest	Acadian Forest
Niagara Forest	Rocky Mountain Forest
Columbia Forest	Mountain Forest
Pacific Coast Forest	Alpine Forest

The Arctic Tundra Region has a very few trees due to a lack of moisture, poor soil and a cold climate. Four major plant communities are found in the Arctic Tundra region. They are rock desert, tundra-heath, strand and freshwater. Lichens are the best known plants. A variety of Arctic flowers such as Arctic poppies, saxifrage and mountain avens can be seen during the summer. They create a colourful landscape.

The Subarctic or Transition Forest Region is the transition stage where open forest and stunted growth create the "land of the little sticks".

The Taiga or Boreal Forest Region consists of white and black spruce, balsam, fir and jack pine which grow in the eastern and central areas, while alpine fir and lodgepole pine are found in the west and northwest.

The Pacific Coast Forest Region has large coniferous trees due to the mild, humid climate. The main species are western red cedar, western hemlock, sitka spruce and Douglas fir.

The Columbia Forest Region is found in the Selkirk and Monashee Mountains. This area is quite wet and the trees are similar to the ones that grow in the Pacific Coast Forest.

The Mountain Forest Region is composed of grassland and scattered stands of Ponderosa Pine. This type of forest grows in the valleys of the central plateau of British Columbia where drought conditions are often experienced.

The Rocky Mountain Forest Region is found on the foothills and the lower mountain slopes. The main species are Engelmann spruce and alpine fir, lodgepole pine and aspen. These forests are mainly used for pulp and paper.

The Alpine Forest Region includes all the mountain areas above the tree line. Meadow and tundra-like plants are quite common in this area.

The Mixed Woods Region is found near the Interior Boreal Region. White spruce, aspen and balm of Gilead are the species found in this region.

The Parkland is a transition area between the forest proper and the prairie grassland. Aspen are seen in scattered patches in the open grassland.

The Prairies Region is divided into a short-grass zone and a mixed grass zone. The types of grasses that grow depend upon the amount of available moisture in the ground. Prairie grasses form a tough sod since they have dense root systems that search for water in the soil. Grasses such as blue gamma grass, common spear grass, western wheat grass, prairie blue grass and June grass are common. Sage brush and prickly pear cactus also grow in the region.

The Great Lakes-St. Lawrence Forest contains a wealth of species. This region's climatic conditions and accessibility make these forests one of the most valuable timber resources. This region supports conifers as well as deciduous trees. Conifers are white pine, red pine and white spruce. Deciduous trees found are sugar maple, beech, red oak and red maple.

The Niagara Region is the eastern deciduous forest region. Species that grow in the Great Lakes-St. Lawrence Forest Region grow here as well as black walnut, scarlet oak, sassafras, magnolia, tulip tree, sycamore and Kentucky coffee tree which usually grows in more southern climates.

The Acadian Forest of Nova Scotia, Prince Edward Island and southern New Brunswick is similar to the Great Lakes Forest region. White spruce, white pine, red pine and red spruce are types of conifers found as well as deciduous hardwoods such as maple, beech and birch.

The Vegetation Regions of Canada

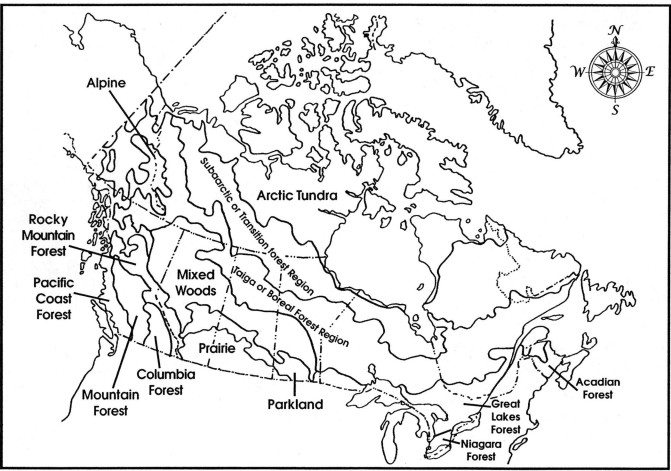

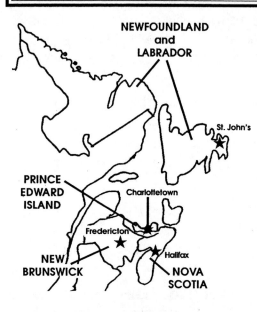

The Atlantic Region is found on the east coast of Canada. It was the first area of Canada to be explored and settled. The Atlantic Region consists of four provinces: Newfoundland and Labrador, New Brunswick, Nova Scotia and Prince Edward Island. The Gaspé and Anticosti Island are also part of this region. New Brunswick and Nova Scotia form part of Canada's mainland. Newfoundland and Labrador consists of the Island and Labrador on the mainland. The Atlantic Region covers five percent of the total area of Canada which is 540 303 square kilometres.

The Gulf of St. Lawrence is surrounded by the Atlantic Region. The Atlantic Ocean is found on its eastern and southern edge. No part of this region is far from the sea. Four large islands are found in the Atlantic Region. They are Newfoundland, Cape Breton Island, Anticosti Island and Prince Edward Island. Nova Scotia and the Gaspé are peninsulas. A peninsula is an area of land almost completely surrounded by water.

Most of the Atlantic Region is made up of the Appalachian Region which consists of low rolling hills except for Prince Edward Island, which is flat and sandy, and Labrador and Labrador, which belongs to the Canadian Shield. The main farming areas in the region are in the Annapolis Lowlands, the Saint John River Valley and Prince Edward Island, as most of the soil in the rest of the region is poor and not suited for agriculture.

Fish and fish processing were major industries in the Atlantic Region until the decline in the fish population on the Grand Banks and in other places of the Atlantic Ocean. The Grand Banks is an area of shallow water southeast of Newfoundland and Labrador. It was once the largest fishing grounds in the world. Other products such as lobsters and scallops are still fished from the sea. New Brunswick and Prince Edward Island are famous for their potatoes. Apples are grown in the Annapolis Valley. Forestry and the manufacture of pulp and paper employ many people. Iron ore and coal are still mined in some areas. Manufacturing is now the leading industry. Tourism has grown rapidly as visitors enjoy the rustic beauty and scenery of the region and its quiet, peaceful charm.

During the winter, the coastal areas of the region experience snowy and stormy weather. During the summer it is mild, wet and often foggy. Icebergs are often carried by the Labrador current to the east coast of Newfoundland and Labrador and keep the air cool until the end of May. Newfoundland and Labrador averages more than one hundred days of fog a year. Inland areas in New Brunswick and the Gaspé experience colder winters and warmer summers.

Only nine per cent of Canada's people live in the Atlantic Provinces. The total population of the region is 2 285 729 (2001 statistics). More than half of the people live in the cities and towns along the coasts. The three largest cities in the region are Halifax in Nova Scotia, Saint John in New Brunswick and St. John's in Newfoundland and Labrador. Each Atlantic Province has a capital city. The capital cities are St. John's, Newfoundland and Labrador; Charlottetown, Prince Edward Island; Fredericton, New Brunswick and Halifax, Nova Scotia.

THE ATLANTIC PROVINCES

#16 Worksheet

Location

1. The province of **Nova Scotia** consists of two main parts – a mainland _____ and an _____ called _____ Island. The island is connected to the mainland by the _____ Causeway. The province of Nova Scotia is joined to the province of New Brunswick by the isthmus of _____.

2. The province of **New Brunswick** has the following sea boundaries:
   a) north _____
   b) south _____
   c) east _____
   Its land boundary on the west is the state of _____. To the north is _____ and to the south is _____.

3. **Prince Edward Island** is the _____ province in Canada. It is surrounded by water. To the northeast its water boundary is the _____, and to the west its water boundary is the _____. Today Prince Edward Island is connected to the mainland of New Brunswick by a _____ that is _____ kilometres in length. It connects _____ on Prince Edward Island and _____ in New Brunswick.

4. **Newfoundland and Labrador** is bounded on the south, east and north by the _____ _____ and on the west by the _____ and _____ _____. The province of Newfoundland and Labrador consists of an _____ and the _____ called Labrador.

Land Surface

Use an atlas that has various types of maps to locate the answers to these activities.

1. Name two important landforms found in Nova Scotia.
   a) _____ b) _____
2. Name two low mountain ranges located in Nova Scotia.
   a) _____ b) _____
3. Name a famous fruit-growing valley found in Nova Scotia.
   a) _____

4. The greater part of New Brunswick consists of the _____
Mountains. These mountains are _____ hills that rise 300 to 800 metres
above sea level. _____ areas are found along the coast.

5. Newfoundland and Labrador's mainland is covered with the _____
and its island consists of the _____ Mountains which are mainly low hills.

6. Name three mountain ranges in Newfoundland and Labrador.
a) _____ b) _____
c) _____

Climate

1. The cold _____ Current is responsible for extensive fog and clouds in
spring and early summer along the coast of the Atlantic provinces.

2. The heaviest rainfall occurs along the outer coast of _____.

3. Newfoundland and Labrador averages more than _____ _____
days of fog a year.

4. New Brunswick's inland areas experience _____ winters and _____
summers.

Waterways

1. The narrow strip of land connecting Nova Scotia to New Brunswick is called an
_____.

2. This narrow strip of land separates two bodies of water, called the _____
and the _____.

3. The cold ocean current coming from the north and making summers cooler in the
Atlantic provinces is called the _____.

4. The warm ocean current coming from the south and making the winters not so cold is
the _____.

5. In which province is each of the following rivers located:

a) Exploits River _____ f) Churchill River _____

b) Petitcodiac River _____ g) Shubernacadie River _____

c) Miramichi _____ h) Annapolis River _____

d) Saint John River _____ i) East River _____

e) Kennebecasis River _____

#16 Worksheet — THE ATLANTIC PROVINCES

Agriculture

1. Why are the Atlantic Provinces for the most part not suitable to agriculture?

   _____

2. Which Atlantic Province is the most suitable for agriculture?

   _____

3. Choose words from the box to complete each sentence.

potatoes	apples	fruit farming	general farming	fur farming
subsistence farming	dairy farming	field crops	Prince Edward Island	

a) _____ means a farmer only grows enough food for his own use and makes no profit from his land.

b) The Annapolis-Cornwallis Valley in Nova Scotia is the only large area used for _____ in the Atlantic Provinces.

c) The main crop of the St. John Valley area in New Brunswick is _____. They are also grown extensively in _____.

d) When a farmer does not specialize in any crop, but grows wheat, oats or hay or keeps cows, pigs and poultry the farming is called _____.

e) _____ are the main fruit grown in the Annapolis Valley.

f) _____ had its beginning in Prince Edward Island and now is found on the western shore of Nova Scotia.

g) Such crops as wheat, clover, hay and oats are called _____.

h) One often finds _____ near large cities because of the good markets there.

Mineral Resources

1. List the important minerals found in the Atlantic Provinces.

   _____
   _____

2. Where is coal mined in Nova Scotia?

   _____

3. The chief coal field in New Brunswick is situated near _____.

4. In which province are there iron-ore mines? _____

5. Where are the iron-ore mines located?

   _____
   _____

THE ATLANTIC PROVINCES

Fishing

1. Choose words from the box to complete the sentences.

continental shelf	cod	Grand Banks	fishing boat,
Atlantic salmon	trawler	dragger	indented coastline

a) When a part of the continent has been submerged beneath the sea it is called a
_____.

b) A large part of the continental shelf, about fifty fathoms deep, lies off the coast of the Atlantic Provinces and is called the _____.

c) At one time _____ and _____ were caught in great abundance off the Grand Banks.

d) Fishing ports are numerous in the Atlantic Provinces because the
_____.

e) If a fisher was going deep-sea fishing he would use either a _____, a _____ or a _____.

2. Name six types of fish or seafood caught in the Atlantic Provinces.

_____   _____

_____   _____

_____   _____

3. Since there has been a moritorium on cod and Atlantic Salmon fishing,
_____ and _____ _____ raise salmon, rainbow trout, mussels and oysters.

4. Many people in the Atlantic Provinces are employed _____,
_____, _____ and _____ fish.

5. Name three countries to which the Atlantic Provinces sell their fish.

_____   _____

_____

Cities in the Atlantic Provinces

1. The most important and only city in Prince Edward Island is _____.
It is situated on a bay which leads into the _____. Its founders decided that it was an excellent place for a city because of its well protected _____. It is the _____ city of Prince Edward Island.

2. The capital city of Nova Scotia is _____. It is situated on the _____ shore of Nova Scotia about half-way between the Strait of _____ and Cape _____. It is known for its large natural _____, big enough for large ocean _____.

3. The capital of New Brunswick is _____ which is situated on the _____ River.

4. The largest and oldest city in New Brunswick is _____ _____. It is located at the mouth of the _____ _____ River where it empties into the _____ of _____. Like many other large cities in the Atlantic Provinces, its excellent _____ was a large factor in deciding its location.

5. The largest city in Newfoundland and Labrador is _____. It is found on the east coast of the _____ Peninsula. St. John's is one of the oldest cities of North America. It is also Newfoundland and Labrador's _____ city.

6. _____ and _____ have paper mills which supply much of the world's newsprint.

8. On a map of the Atlantic Provinces locate and label the following. The names of the waterways are to be printed in the boxes. The names of the provinces are to be printed on the double lines. The names of cities and town are to be printed on the lines beside the dots.

Waterways

Atlantic Ocean; Gulf of St. Lawrence; Bay of Fundy;
Cabot Strait; Strait of Canso; Strait of Belle Isle; Saint John River

Provinces

Newfoundland and Labrador; New Brunswick; Nova Scotia; Prince Edward Island

Cities and Towns

Fredericton	Halifax	Cornerbrook	Borden
Charlottetown	St. John's	Edmundston	Yarmouth
Sydney	Lunenburg	Truro	Grand Falls
Moncton	Souris	Saint John	Gander

The Symbols of the Atlantic Provinces

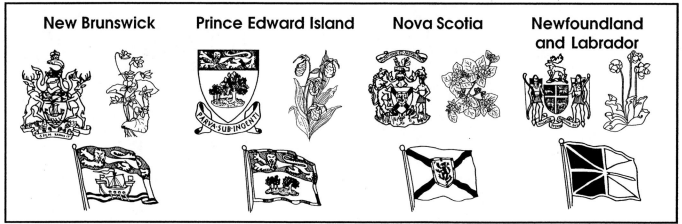

Map of the Atlantic Provinces

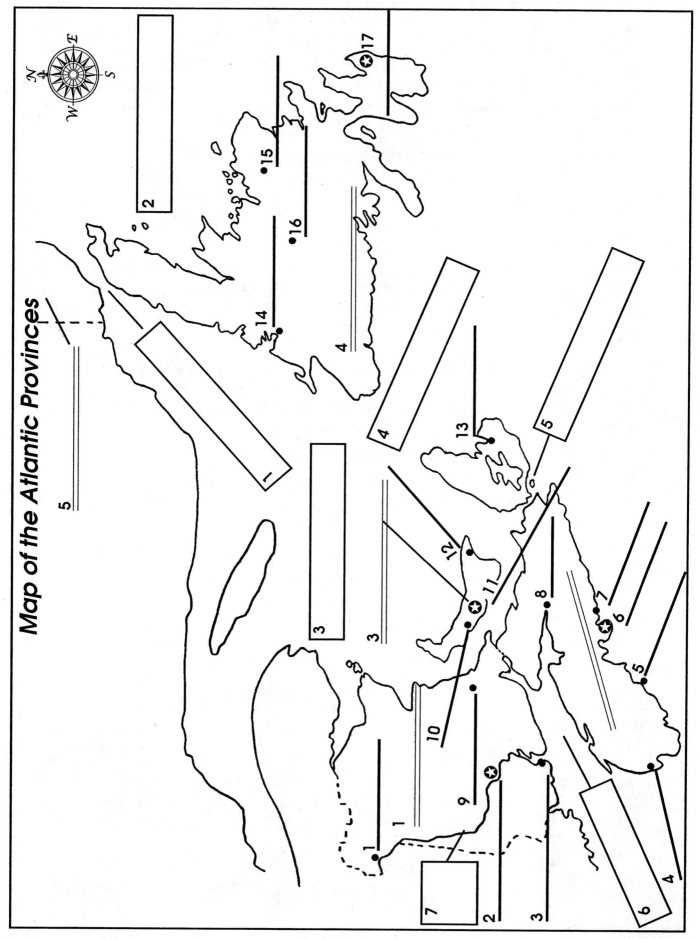

SSJ1-38

QUÉBEC

Québec is the largest province in Canada covering 1 540 630 square kilometres of its land. Québec City is the oldest city in Canada and it is also the provincial capital. Montréal is the largest city in Québec and one of the busiest. The word Québec came from the Algonquin word "kebec" which means "the place where the river narrows". The French explorer, Samuel de Champlain, heard the native people use this word to describe a place on the St. Lawrence River. It is at this place where he built a settlement and founded Québec City in 1608. It was the first permanent settlement in Canada.

The province of Québec ranks the second highest in population next to Ontario. There are 7 237 479 people (2001 census) living in Québec. Eighty per cent of the people in Québec are French Canadian and speak French. The strong French influence makes Québec unique and quite different from the rest of the provinces and territories. Ninety per cent of the people belong to the Roman Catholic church. Most children are instructed in French and receive instruction pertaining to religion. Ten per cent of the people are of British descent. A large number of First Nations People live in northern Québec as well.

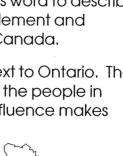

Québec has four main land regions:
1. The Canadian Shield
2. The St. Lawrence Lowlands
3. The Appalachian Region
4. The Hudson Bay Lowlands

The Canadian Shield covers nine-tenths of the province. It includes the North Shore which extends along the St. Lawrence River from the Saguenay River to Labrador. Most of the ancient rocks in this region have little or no soil at all. This area is a wilderness of forests, lakes, rivers and streams. This region has little land that can be farmed but it does have a variety of mineral deposits.

The St. Lawrence Lowlands consists of the St. Lawrence River Valley and the Montréal Plain. The lowlands are about sixteen kilometres wide near Québec City and broaden to one hundred kilometres at Montréal. The fertile soil in this valley supports most of Québec's farming. Québec is a leading producer of dairy cattle, hogs, milk and maple syrup. This area is one of the most heavily populated regions of Canada.

The Appalachian Region extends from Vermont along the province's southeastern boundary. This area is heavily forested, mountainous and dotted with lakes and streams. The Hudson Bay Lowlands extends into Québec from Ontario. It covers a small strip of land south of James Bay.

Québec's coastline is 13 773 kilometres in length and includes bays, inlets and offshore islands. The main bodies of water that surround Québec are: James and Hudson Bays on the west, Hudson Strait and Ungava Bay on the north, and the Gulf of St. Lawrence on the southeast and south.

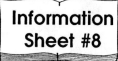
The climate in Québec varies greatly. Its winters are long and cold and its summers are warm but short. During the winter, southern Québec can receive 246 to 422 centimetres of snow between November and mid-March.

Québec is a leading manufacturer and produces about a fourth of all the goods manufactured in Canada. Most of the paper in North America is produced in Québec. It is a leader in the production of hydro-electric power due to its abundant supply of water power. Québec's natural resources provide many of its industries with valuable raw materials. The abundant forests supply its growing paper industry.

Québec's rich history, rugged terrain, beautiful lakes and rolling farmland attract tourists and outdoor sporting enthusiasts yearly. Tourism is a growing trade in Québec.

Symbols of Québec

QUÉBEC

Location

Québec is a large triangle of land found in the _____ corner of North America. It is bordered by _____ to the west; _____ to the east; _____, _____, and _____ State to the south; and _____ to the north. It is the _____ province in Canada.

Surface

Québec has four main regions. They are the _____, the _____, the _____, and the _____.

The St. Lawrence Lowlands is a _____ _____ of land along the St. Lawrence River. This area contains the province's most _____ land. _____ per cent of the people of this province live here.

The Appalachian Highlands are a low _____ _____ that lies between the St. Lawrence River and the American Border.

The Canadian Shield Region is also known as the _____. It covers ninety percent of Québec.

The Hudson Bay Lowlands cover a small strip of land south of _____.

Climate

Québec's climate _____ greatly. Its winters are _____ and _____. A winter can last for _____ to _____ days. The cold winds from the North Pole collide with warm winds from the south causing much _____ and varied _____. In the southern part of Québec summers can be _____ and _____.

Rivers of Québec

Using an atlas, locate the following rivers found on a map of Québec.

1. The river that forms part of the boundary between Ontario and Québec is the

   _____

2. The four chief tributaries of the St. Lawrence River are

   _____

   _____

3. Six rivers which flow north are

   _____

   _____

   _____

       SSJ1-38

4. Four rivers flowing west are

_____

_____

5. The Saguenay River starts from _____ .

6. The source of the Leaf River (Rivière aux Feuilles) is _____ .

7. The body of water into which the Fort George River empties is _____ .

8. A southern tributary of the St. Lawrence River is _____ .

Agriculture in Québec

1. Québec is one of the great agricultural provinces of Canada and is known for its
   _____ farming. There are more than _____ farms in Québec
   mainly along the _____ and over _____ of them are
   dairy farms. They supply milk for the making of _____ and _____ .

2. Name four types of grains grown in Québec.

   _____

3. What fruits are grown on Québec's farms?

   _____

4. What vegetables are grown on Québec's farms?

   _____

   _____

5. Québec farmers also raise _____, _____
   and _____ .

6. Québec is famous all over the world for its _____ _____ and
   _____ _____ which come from the _____ of maple trees.

Québec's Industries

1. List the major industries found in Québec.

   _____   _____

   _____   _____

   _____   _____

   _____   _____

2. The main industry in Québec is the production of _____ .
   It is the largest producer of _____ in Canada.

3. Québec has the fifth largest _____ _____ in the world.

4. The world's largest copper smelter is located in _____ .

5. Iron ore is mined at _____ and along the Québec-Labrador border.

6. Gold is mined at _____ and _____ .

7. Québec is the leading producer of _____. It also produces all of Canada's _____ which is used in paint.

Québec's Cities

1. _____ _____ is the capital city of the Province of Québec. It is the only _____ city in North America and the _____ city in Canada. It was founded by a French explorer named _____ in 1608. It is an important _____ and _____ attraction.

2. _____ is the largest city in Québec. It is located on an _____ in the St. Lawrence River. It is a _____ tourist attraction for visitors.

3. _____ is known as "paper town" as it produces ten per cent of the world's paper. It is located on the St. Lawrence River _____ between Montréal and Québec City.

4. Look at a map of Québec and locate the names of eight cities and towns.

_____   _____
_____   _____
_____   _____
_____   _____

Map Work

On a map of the Province of Québec locate the following places. The names of waterways are to be printed in the boxes. The names of provinces are to be printed in the circles. The names of cities and towns are to be printed on the lines beside the dots.

Waterways

St. Lawrence River	Ottawa River	Strait of Jacques Cartier
Ungava Bay	Strait of Honguedo	Strait of Belle Isle
Hudson Strait	James Bay	Hudson Bay

Cities and Towns

Québec City	Gaspé	Montréal
Sherbrooke	Hull	Trois Rivières
Sept-Iles	Rimouski	Rivière du Loup
Rouyn	Val d'Or	

Provinces

New Brunswick	Newfoundland
Ontario	Québec

Map of Quebec

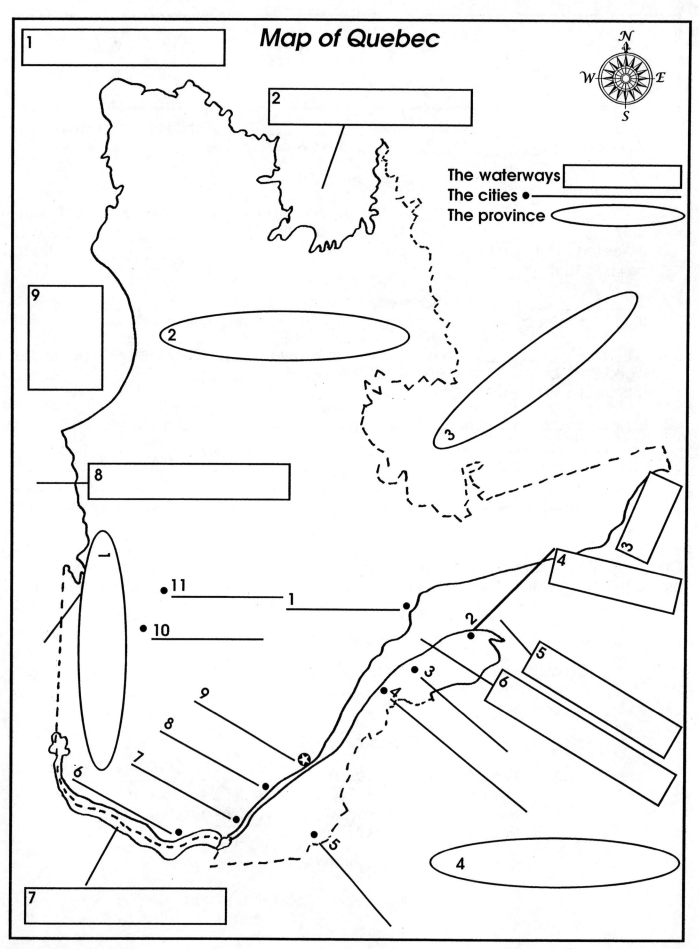

The waterways
The cities ●
The province

Of all the provinces of Canada Ontario is the second largest in area. It covers 1 068 580 square kilometres of our country. It is the southernmost province but it also extends so far north that some of its ground beneath the surface is permafrost (permanently frozen). Ontario's name comes from the Iroquois Native people. It may mean "beautiful lake" or "rocks standing high" or "near the water", which refer to Niagara Falls. Its capital city is Toronto which lies on the northwest shore of Lake Ontario. It is one of the busiest Canadian ports on the Great Lakes. Ottawa, the capital city of Canada, is also found in Ontario and is located on the Ottawa River.

Ontario has the largest population of all the provinces: 11 410 046 (2001 census). Most of the people live in 12 percent of the province's land area. Ontario is heavily populated mainly in the southernmost part near the Great Lakes and the larger cities. Ontario has 38 cities with a population of 50 000 or more. No other Canadian province has so many large cities. Ontario's population has become very multicultural and consists of people from all over the world.

Ontario has four main land regions. They are the Hudson Bay Lowlands, the Canadian Shield, the St. Lawrence Lowlands and the Great Lakes Lowlands.

The Hudson Bay Lowlands curves around the southern part of Hudson Bay and extends as far south as Kesagami Lake. This region is flat and poorly drained, and large muskegs (peat bogs) are located in it. A narrow belt of permafrost (permanently frozen ground) is found in this lowland near the Arctic.

The Canadian Shield, a low rocky region, covers more than half of Ontario. The Canadian Shield is located below the Hudson Bay Lowlands and stretches to a narrow area along Lake Ontario. This region is filled with many small lakes and rivers surrounded by forests. The Canadian Shield is rich in gamelife, minerals and timber. A large area called the clay belt, which extends from Hearst to the Québec border supports a variety of crops grown by farmers and provides grassland for grazing beef and dairy cattle.

The St. Lawrence Lowlands runs along the St. Lawrence River. It is a wedge-shaped area located between the Ottawa and St. Lawrence Rivers. It contains low hills and fertile valleys. Fruits, grains and vegetables are grown here, and dairy cattle are raised extensively.

The Great Lakes Lowlands lies along much of the Great Lakes in Ontario. It touches Lakes Erie, Huron, St. Clair and Ontario. The soil here is very fertile and in many areas the land is flat. The Niagara Escarpment is a high cliff or ridge that extends 402 kilometres from Manitoulin Island through the Bruce Peninsula to Niagara Falls. The escarpment forms a shelter for Ontario's best fruit-growing belt.

Ontario's inland shoreline stretches 8 452 kilometres along the many bays, inlets and sandy beaches of Lakes Erie, Ontario, Huron, and Superior. Manitoulin Island, found in Lake Huron, is the largest inland island in the world. It has an area of 2 765 square kilometres.

ONTARIO

Ontario has over 400 000 lakes, countless streams, rivers and waterfalls sprinkled throughout the province. The St. Lawrence River and the Great Lakes provide a natural highway for many ocean-going vessels into the interior of Canada. Hydro-electric plants on the Niagara River and other rivers provide Ontario with an abundant source of power.

Southern Ontario has a milder climate than the rest of the province. Winds from the Great Lakes moderate its climate. Northern Ontario experiences cold air waves from the Arctic or the Prairies. During the winter, the temperature and the amount of snow fall vary throughout the season. The summers are warmer in Southern Ontario than in Northern Ontario.

Ontario's manufacturing industries make it one of the richest economic regions of North America. Industrial workers produce half of the country's manufactured products. Toronto is Canada's leading industrial centre. Major manufacturing industries produce vehicles, chemicals, food and beverages, electrical products, metal products, paper products and printed materials.

Agriculture is an important industry. There are approximately 68 000 farms in the province which use five percent of the land area and each farm is an average of 80 hectares in size. Ontario is the leading produce of fruits and vegetables especially in the famous Niagara fruit belt. Beef and dairy farming produce many products sold throughout the province and Canada.

Mining in Ontario produces more than a third of Canada's most valuable mineral products. Sudbury, Cochran, Kenora and Thunder Bay are important mining centres.

Electricity is produced in Ontario's nuclear power plants, fuel-burning power plants and hydro-electric plants. Ontario Hydro, which operates many hydro-electric plants, is a large publicly owned utility.

Ontario is known as the industrial heartland of Canada.

Symbols of Ontario

ONTARIO

Location

1. Name the boundaries of Ontario. Begin at the north-east and proceed in a clock-wise direction.

   _____

   _____

2. Approximately how much of the boundaries are water? _____

3. Which of the Great Lakes is not a boundary of Ontario? _____

4. What is the most southerly point of Ontario? _____

5. Although Ontario is an inland province, why are ocean vessels able to travel to its main cities.

   _____

   _____

6. On the accompanying map, mark in and name the boundaries of Ontario. Trace the boundary lines in red.

Surface

1. Ontario has _____ main geographic regions. They are: _____

   _____

   _____ .

2. The Hudson Bay Lowlands curve around the southern part of _____ and _____. This area is _____, poorly _____ and has large _____ (peat bogs). In some areas there is _____ (permanently frozen land).

3. The Canadian Shield is a very large _____ -shaped region that covers most of Ontario. It is a _____ region containing many _____ and _____ areas. Large rich _____ areas allow farmers to raise a variety of crops such as _____ and _____. Farmers are able to raise _____ and _____ also on the _____. This area is also rich in _____, _____ and _____.

4. The St. Lawrence Lowlands runs along the _____.
   It is a _____ area wedged between the Ottawa and St. Lawrence Rivers. The soil is _____ and farmers grow fruits and vegetables and large _____ farms are found there.

5. The Great Lakes Lowlands lie along much of the _____ in Canada. This region touches Lakes _____, _____ and _____. The grey-brown soil is very _____ and many different kinds of _____ are grown. _____ and _____ cattle are also raised.

71   SSJ1-38

Map of Ontario's Boundaries

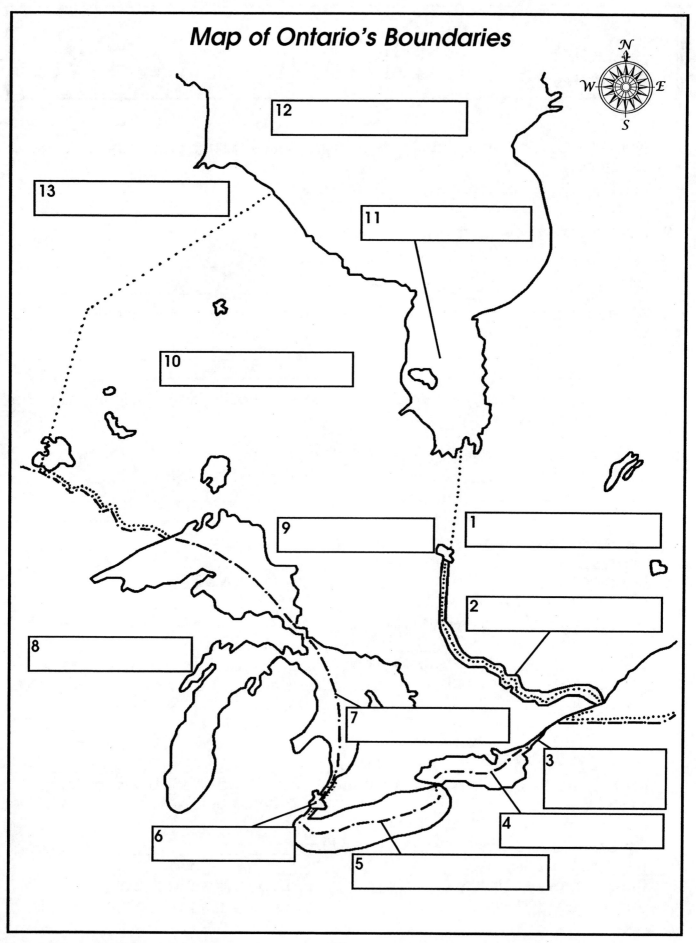

ONTARIO

The _____ is found in this region. It is a high _____
or _____ that runs for 402 kilometres from _____
through the _____ to Niagara Falls. This escarpment is
a _____ _____ for Ontario's best fruit growing area.
Canada's _____ cities are found in the Great Lakes Lowlands.

Climate

1. All of Ontario has four distinct seasons. They are _____, _____,
   _____, and _____.

2. _____ Ontario has a much _____ climate than _____
   Ontario due to the _____ from the Great Lakes. Northern Ontario is
   usually _____ in all the seasons.

3. The average winter temperature can range from _____ in Southern Ontario to
   _____ in Northern Ontario. The average midsummer temperature can be
   _____ in the province's far north and _____ in its south.

4. The average rainfall for the province is _____ per year. Some
   parts of Southern Ontario receive _____ that much. Some areas in
   Northern Ontario receive up to 300 centimetres of snow a year.

Lakes and Rivers of Ontario

Underline the correct answers:

1. The largest lake in or bordering Ontario is (Lake Nipigon, Lake Superior, Lake Simcoe, Lake Huron).

2. The smallest lake of the following group is (Lake Erie, Lake Nipigon, Lake Ontario, Lake St. Clair)

3. Lake (Huron, Nipissing, Ontario) flows directly into the St. Lawrence River.

4. An ocean vessel can not enter (Lake Ontario, Lake of the Woods, Rainy Lake, Lake Superior)

5. The (Ottawa River, St. Clair River, Albany River) joins Lake St. Clair and Lake Huron.

6. The (St. Lawrence River, Niagara River, French River) joins Lake Ontario with Lake Erie.

7. The (Abitibi River, Nipigon River, Detroit River) flows into James Bay.

8. The (Rainy River, Ottawa River, Thames River) flows into the St. Lawrence River.

9. The (St. Mary's River, Trent River, Humber River) joins Lake Huron with Lake Superior.

10. The (Grand River, Madawaska River, Severn River) flows into the Ottawa River.

11. The (Rideau River, Detroit River, Nelson River) joins Lake St. Clair with Lake Erie.

12. The (Rainy River, Thames River, Severn River) flows north into Hudson Bay.

ONTARIO

Agriculture

1. Ontario is Canada's _____ agricultural producer. In Ontario, crops such as hay, oats, mixed grains and corn are grown by farmers to feed their _____. In Southern Ontario _____ is the main crop grown.

2. _____ farming produces many products such as _____, _____, _____, _____, _____ and _____.

3. The raising of livestock for _____ and _____ has increased in Ontario.

4. Specialty farms are found in the _____ region. This area is famous for its _____, _____, _____, _____, _____ and other fruit. Many _____ have developed in this growing area.

5. Four _____ in Southern Ontario were drained so _____ could be grown. They are the _____, _____, _____ and the _____.

Forestry

1. In Ontario the _____ owns almost all of the forest land. The government sells _____ to private companies to _____ areas of forest.

2. Trees that are cut are used for _____ and to make _____ and _____. There are about _____ pulp and paper mills located in Ontario and most are found in the _____ part. The mills are located near major _____ and near large bodies of water such as Lakes _____, _____ and _____.

   _____, a thin layer of wood made from hardwood trees, is manufactured in _____ and _____. _____ is made from poplar trees in _____ and _____. Particle board is made at mills in _____, _____ and _____.

3. Name two kinds of forests found in Ontario.
   a) _____   b) _____

4. Give two reasons why waterways are important in the lumbering industry.
   a) _____
   _____
   b) _____
   _____

ONTARIO

Mining

1. The Canadian Shield is very rich in _____.

2. Name nine minerals that are found in Ontario.

   _____ _____ _____
   _____ _____ _____
   _____ _____ _____

3. Name the two main minerals produced in Ontario.

   a) _____ b) _____

4. What mineral is produced in Sudbury? _____

5. What mineral is produced at Timmins? _____

6. Which valuable mineral is mined at Timmins, Kirkland Lake and Red Lake? _____

Industries

1. Tell why Ontario has become a great industrial province.

   _____
   _____
   _____
   _____
   _____
   _____
   _____

2. What is the most important industrial area in the province?

   _____
   _____

3. Steel-making has been a leading industry in Ontario for a long time. Steel-making takes place in _____ and _____.

4. The _____ industry provides many Ontarians with work. Many factories make _____ for cars and trucks.

5. _____ production is the second highest manufacturing activity in Ontario.

6. The _____ of _____ and _____ is the third highest manufacturing activity in Ontario. _____, _____ _____ and _____ are the leading beverages produced. Food plants process _____, _____, _____ and _____ products. Ontario _____ process _____ into _____, and other _____ are used for _____.

ONTARIO

Cities and Towns

Name the centre in Ontario where each of these industries take place.

1. It is the centre of atomic energy. _____

2. They are the four, main, important lake ports. _____
_____

3. It has a nickel refinery. _____

4. They are two cities that manufacture breakfast foods. _____
_____

5. There are five cities that manufacture cars in Ontario. _____
_____

6. It is an important hydro-electric centre. _____

7. There are eight centres that all have universities. _____
_____
_____

8. These two cities are important steel-making centres. _____
_____

9. It is home to the provincial government of Ontario. _____

10. It is the centre where the federal government is held. _____

Mapping Activity

On the map of Ontario locate and neatly label the following cities.

Hamilton	**Niagara Falls**	**Sudbury**	**Kingston**
North Bay	**Timmins**	**Kirkland Lake**	**Ottawa**
Thunder Bay	**London**	**Pembroke**	**Timmins**
Moose Factory	**Sault Ste Marie**		**Toronto**

Map of Ontario

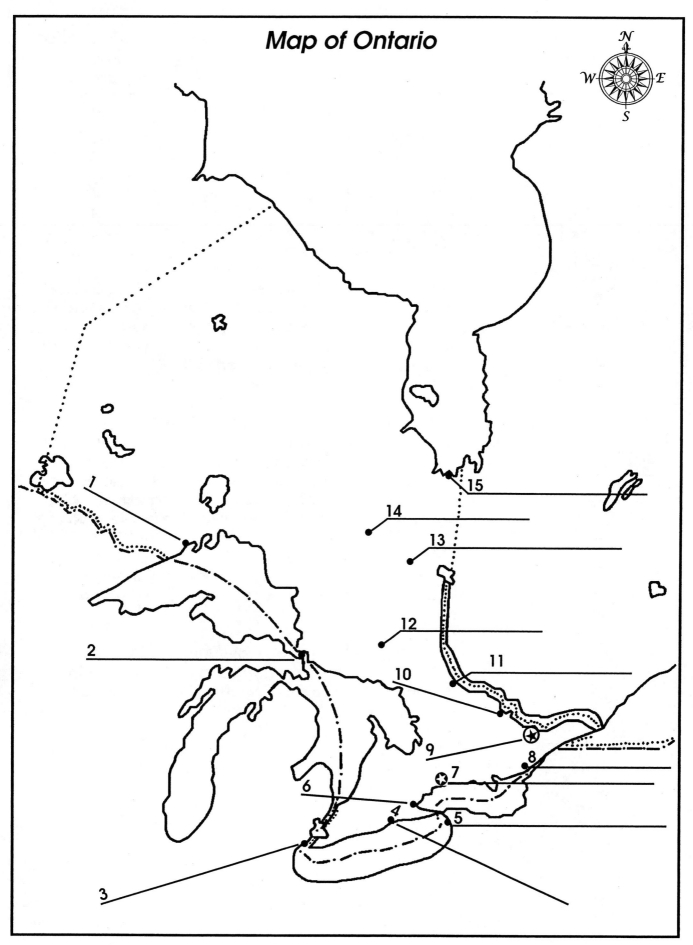

SSJ1-38

THE PRAIRIE PROVINCES

Manitoba

Saskatchewan

Alberta

The provinces of Manitoba, Saskatchewan and Alberta make up the prairie region. Manitoba has three main physical features. They are the Hudson Bay Lowlands, The Canadian Shield and the first level of the Interior Plain or Plateau. Saskatchewan consists of the second level of the Interior Plain or Plateau. Alberta is entirely made up of the third level of the Interior Plain or Plateau. Each level of the Interior Plain becomes progressively higher as you proceed from east to west.

Located in the southern part of each province is a large triangular-shaped land area called a "prairie". A prairie is a large grassland with very few trees. Canada's prairie region stretches from the foothills of the Rocky Mountains in the west to the Red River in the east. The northern area of each province is covered with evergreen forests.

The three Prairie Provinces occupy 1 963 470 square kilometres of Canada's land area. The population in the prairie region is 5 073 323 (2001 census). Most of the people live in the southern part of each province or the prairie area. Large wheat farms are found here as the land is very fertile and flat. Cattle ranching is found on the drier, hilly parts of the prairie region.

The Prairie Provinces are also rich in minerals. Oil and gas wells are seen throughout this region. Nickel and copper mines are found in the north. Potash is also mined and used to make fertilizer.

Each province has a capital city: Winnipeg, Manitoba; Regina, Saskatchewan; Edmonton, Alberta. The provincial government for each province is found in each capital city. Other cities are Calgary and Saskatoon.

The prairie region experiences a much drier climate than other regions of Canada. The Rocky Mountains block the moist winds from the Pacific Ocean causing the air to be dry. Winters are long, windy and very cold but often sunny and very bright. During the summer the rain falls as showers and the amount varies from year to year. Some years can be too dry and other years may be too wet. Summers are usually warm and sunny.

The prairie region is very rich in agricultural and mineral resources. Three quarters of Canada's total cropland is in this area.

THE PRAIRIE PROVINCES

Location

1. Give the boundaries of:
   a) **Manitoba:**
   North Border - _____
   West Border - _____
   East Border - _____
   South Border - _____

   b) **Saskatchewan:**
   North Border - _____
   West Border - _____
   East Border - _____
   South Border - _____

   c) **Alberta:**
   North Border - _____
   West Border - _____
   East Border - _____
   South Border - _____

Surface

1. What is a slough? _____
   _____

2. The Prairie Provinces are each divided into three main physical regions.
   Manitoba contains the _____, _____
   and the first level of the _____ or _____.
   Saskatchewan consists of the second level of the _____ or
   _____.

   Alberta consists of the third level of the _____ or
   _____.

3. What does a prairie look like? _____
   _____

4. Why are there few trees on the prairies? _____
   _____
   _____
   _____

5. What is a drought? _____
   _____
   _____

6. Why can a prairie farmer successfully grow grain in these provinces?

   _____

7. What are the chief causes for crop failure in the Prairie Provinces?

   _____

   _____

Climate

1. **Manitoba's** climate can vary greatly. In the _____ the average temperature may be -19.3 °C in January, and in the summer, in July, it can be as hot as 19.6 °C.

   The _____ of the province receives the most precipitation and the _____ receives the least.

   Manitoba enjoys plenty of _____ all year long. It is one of North America's _____ spots.

   In the northern part of the province the summers are so _____ that _____ stays in the ground year-round. This is called _____.

   In _____ Manitoba, the land is quite flat and a fast _____ melt or too much spring _____ causes the rivers and streams to _____ their banks and _____ the countryside.

   What is the name of the river in Manitoba that did overflow its banks in 1950?

   _____

2. **Saskatchewan's** climate is quite _____. It suffers from _____, bitterly _____ winters and _____, extremely _____ summers. Spring and fall are quite _____. There is a constant _____ during all the seasons. Saskatachewan's climate is known as _____ with low_____ and _____ on the plains and lots of _____.

   The plains area often suffers from _____. In _____ Saskatchewan winters are much _____ with temperatures around - 40 °C.

3. **Alberta** has a very _____ climate. It has been known that near the mountains the weather can change suddenly. In early May, the _____ melts in the mountains, except on the higher peaks, where it stays all summer long. Alberta's warmest months are _____ and _____. July is usually the _____ month. Autumn is beautiful in Alberta as _____ is usually experienced after the first frosts. The days are _____ but the nights are _____. Snow in Alberta lasts for five or six months and comes in _____ and stays until _____.

THE PRAIRIE PROVINCES

In the winter, the prairies receive _____ that are dangerous with a high _____ factor, high _____ and poor _____. The coldest month is _____. Temperatures in the winter can rise or fall _____ depending on the _____. Winds from the _____ cause temperatures to drop. Winds from the _____ and an _____ signal the arrival of a _____.

A chinook is a _____ and _____ wind that raises the temperature as much as _____ degrees Celsius in one hour. Within hours all the snow on the ground will have _____.

Lakes and Rivers

Using your mapping skills underline the correct answers below:

1. The largest lake in the Prairie Provinces is (Lake Athabasca, Cree Lake, Lake Winnipeg, Cedar Lake, Frobisher Lake, Lake Manitoba, Island Lake).

2. The most northerly lake is (God's Lake, Reindeer Lake, Southern Indian Lake, Lake Athabasca, Lac La Ronge, Lake Winnipegosis, Lake Dauphin).

3. The most southerly lake is (Churchill Lake, Lesser Slave Lake, Lake Louise, Lake Manitoba, Moose Lake, Wollaston Lake).

4. Most lakes are located in (Manitobal Saskatchewan, Alberta).

5. Underline the two rivers that flow into Lake Winnipeg: (Peace River, Athabasca River, Hayes River, Dauphin River, Red River) .

6. Which three rivers flow into the Hudson Bay? (Nelson River, Saskatchewan River, Athabasca River, Churchill River, Qu'Appelle River, Hayes River, Winnipeg River, Red River). _____ _____ _____

7. Which river flows through all three Prairie Provinces? _____

Agriculture

1. _____ is **Manitoba's** most important industry. _____ is the main crop grown. Other crops such as _____, _____, _____, _____ and _____ are grown. Manitoba is one of the world's major producer of _____. _____ production is the second largest farming industry. The average size of a farm in Manitoba is _____.

   Manitoba's grain is held in 300 _____ _____ throughout the province. It is a _____ for marketing and transporting grain to other places. Agricultural _____, _____ and _____ are manufactured in the province.

2. **Saskatchewan** is the _____ largest agricultural producer in Canada. It produces immense crops of _____, _____, _____, _____, _____ and _____ _____. It also produces large quantities of _____, _____, _____, _____, _____, _____, _____ and _____. Of all the products produced _____ is still the most important.

An average farm in Saskatchewan is _____ hectares. There are now _____ farms as smaller farms have been bought to form larger ones. Unfortunately in the last _____ years _____ _____ have been low but _____ _____ have been very high. The _____ has to help the farmers during hard times and crop failure.

3. **Alberta's** major agricultural crops produced are _____, _____ and _____. Poultry, _____ and _____ are also produced. Many products are exported to _____ and the _____.

Farms in Alberta are _____. They are getting _____ but _____ in number. Larger farms can use the _____ and expensive _____ more economically. New _____ have been introduced due to low prices for wheat, barley and rye.

4. Why are all the Prairie Provinces suited for farming? Think of four reasons.

_____
_____
_____

Industries

1. **Manitoba's** leading manufactured products are _____, _____, _____ and _____, _____ and _____ and _____.

_____ is the main mineral mined from Manitoba's mines. _____ is the second most important metal. _____ is where most of the province's copper is produced. Other important metals mined are _____, _____, _____, _____, _____, and _____.

Manitoba has plenty of _____ and _____ and is able to produce its own _____-_____ power. Power is produced on the _____, _____ and _____ Rivers.

_____ and _____ are produced near Virden. Pulp and paper are produced at _____ and _____. Located at _____, on the Winnipeg River, is one of Canada's nuclear research centres.

2. **Saskatchewan's** ground is also very rich with _____ and _____. _____ is exported all over the world to make _____. Saskatchewan has three mines that produce _____ and it is the world's largest _____. The province also produces _____, copper, _____, _____, sand, gravel and _____.

Saskatchewan is also a major producer of _____ and _____. _____ and _____ have refineries that process heavy oil. The province has the world's largest reserve of _____ which is a thick, sludgy mixture of oil and sand. It is very expensive to _____ and _____.

_____ coal which burns quickly and gives off less heat is mined in Saskatchewan. It is used at power-generating _____ thoughout the province.

_____ has steadily increased in the province. Many manufacturers are small and produce products such as _____, _____, _____, _____, diapers and enamel pins. One of the largest _____ is located in _____. Other industries include food-processing, printing, machinery, metal products, wood, electric and electronics.

There is some _____ done and _____ and _____ mills are found in the province. This type of industry is relatively _____ even though a large part of Northern Saskatchewan is _____.

Although Saskatchewan is a land-locked area _____ does play an important role. The province has many fresh-water lakes filled with _____, _____, _____ and other fish. Commercial fishers harvest the fish which is sold to the _____ and _____.

3. **Alberta** is known as the _____ _____ due to its abundant _____ resources. Alberta has three types of oil resources such as _____ oil, _____ oil and oil _____. There are two kinds of natural gas such as _____ gas and _____ gas. Sweet gas is the type burned in household _____. The refined gas is _____ to California and other States and _____ to other parts of Canada.

The largest manufacturing business is the _____ and _____ industry. Other industries are clothing, food products, furniture, forest products, _____, _____, telecommunications and _____.

Alberta's _____ industry is rapidly growing and many people are concerned about its effects. The people do not want the forests to become _____. They fear the _____ will allow the public to _____ and _____ the natural forest. There are concerns that _____ and _____ mills will pollute or harm the _____ and _____ Rivers.

People are concerned about the effect that _____ will have on the forest's _____, _____, _____ and _____.

Lumber, pulp, wood preservation products, poles and other wood products are exported to the _____ and the _____ countries. Lumbering areas are found near centres such as

_____, _____, _____, _____, _____, _____, _____, and _____.

Alberta trades with countries such as the _____, _____, _____, _____ and _____. The items traded are _____ and _____ products, _____, _____, _____, _____ and _____. Most of the trade workers are employed in the _____ industry. Edmonton's West Edmonton _____ is internationally known.

_____ is an important industry in Alberta. Its spectacular _____ is found in the _____. _____, _____ and _____ national parks attract millions of tourists from all over the world.

Tourist Attractions

Where in the Prairie Provinces would you find the following? Write the name of the centre and the province or just the name of the province on the line at the end of each activity.

1. the Red Deer Badlands - _____
2. the Snowbirds, Canada's famous flying team - _____

_____

3. real polar bears - _____

4. a famous western Stampede - _____

5. cattle ranches - _____

6. a famous National Park - _____

7. a school for RCMPs - _____

8. rock formations called Hoodoos - _____

9. a gigantic Ukrainian Easter egg - _____

10. glaciers and icefields - _____

11. a salt water harbour - _____

12. a dinosaur museum - _____

13. oil wells in fields pumping oil - _____

14. lots of grain elevators - _____

Manitoba's Cities

1. On the map of Manitoba locate and name the following cities. Locate and name the capital city. It has a star in a circle on the map. Each city is represented by a dot and a line. Print the names neatly on the lines.

Brandon	**St. Boniface**	**Flin Flon**	**Winnipeg**	**Portage La Prairie**
The Pas	**Churchill**	**Selkirk**	**Lynn Lake**	

On the map of Manitoba mark on the following rivers and lakes. Each lake and river is represented by a numeral inside a circle. Print the names neatly on the lines.

Lake Winnipeg	**Lake Manitoba**	**Lake Winnipegosis**	**Winnipeg River**
Assiniboine River	**Churchill River**	**Nelson River**	**Hayes River**
Red River	**Souris River**		

2. Tell why each of these cities is important.

a) Winnipeg: _____

_____

b) Brandon: _____

_____

c) Portage La Prairie: _____

_____

d) Flin Flon: _____

_____

e) The Pas: _____

_____

f) Churchill: _____

_____

g) Souris: _____

_____

#19 Worksheet THE PRAIRIE PROVINCES

Saskatchewan's Cities

1. a) On the accompanying map locate the following cities. The cities are marked with a dot and a line. The capital city is marked with a circled star. Print each name neatly on the line provided.

Regina	**Saskatoon**	**North Battleford**	**Weyburn**
Yorkton	**Uranium City**	**Moose Jaw**	**Swift Current**
Estevan	**Lloydminister**	**Prince Albert**	

   b) Mark on the following lakes and rivers. The lakes and rivers are marked with a numeral inside a circle. Print each river's name neatly on the line and each lake's name neatly in the box provided.

Lake Athabasca	**Wollaston Lake**	**Reindeer lake**
Lac La Ronge	**Qu'Appelle River**	**South Saskatchewan River**
Cree River	**Souris River**	**North Saskatchewan River**

   Colour all the other lakes and rivers blue.

2. The cities below are located on rivers. Locate the city on a map and then locate the river that it's on.

   a) North Battleford is on the ______________________________.
   b) Saskatoon is on the ______________________________.
   c) Prince Albert is on the ______________________________.
   d) Weyburn is on the ______________________________.
   e) Fort Qu'Appelle is on the ______________________________.

3. Tell why each of the following cities is important.

   a) Saskatoon: ______________________________
   ____

   b) Weyburn: ______________________________
   ____
   ____

   c) Estevan: ______________________________
   ____

   d) Regina: ______________________________
   ____

   e) Prince Albert: ______________________________
   ____
   ____

   f) Batouche: ______________________________
   ____

Alberta's Cities

1. a) On the accompanying map, locate the following cities. The cities are marked with a dot. Print each name neatly on the line provided. The capital city is marked with a circled star.

Edmonton	**Lethbridge**	**Red Deer**	**Calgary**
Medicine Hat	**Camrose**	**Grande Prairie**	**Wetaskiwin**
Drumheller	**Lloydminister**	**Banff**	**Jasper**

   b) Name the following lakes and rivers. The lakes and rivers are marked with a numeral inside a circle. Print each name neatly in the box provided or on the line.

Lake Athabaska	**Lake Claire**	**Lesser Slave Lake**	**Utikuma Lake**
Bistcho Lake	**Bow River**	**South Saskatchewan River**	**Athabasca River**
Red Deer River	**Peace River**	**North Saskatchewan River**	

   Colour all the other lakes and rivers blue.

2. The cities below are located on rivers. Locate the city on a map and then locate the river that its on.

   a) Edmonton is on the _____ .

   b) Calgary is on the _____ .

   c) Lethbridge is on the _____ .

   d) Medicine Hat is on the _____ .

   e) Red Deer is on the _____ .

   f) Drumheller is on the _____ .

   g) Fort McMurray is on the _____ .

3. Tell why each of the following cities is important.

   a) Calgary: _____

   b) Banff: _____

   c) Drumheller: _____

   d) Edmonton: _____

   e) Leduc: _____

   f) Vegreville: _____

Map of Manitoba

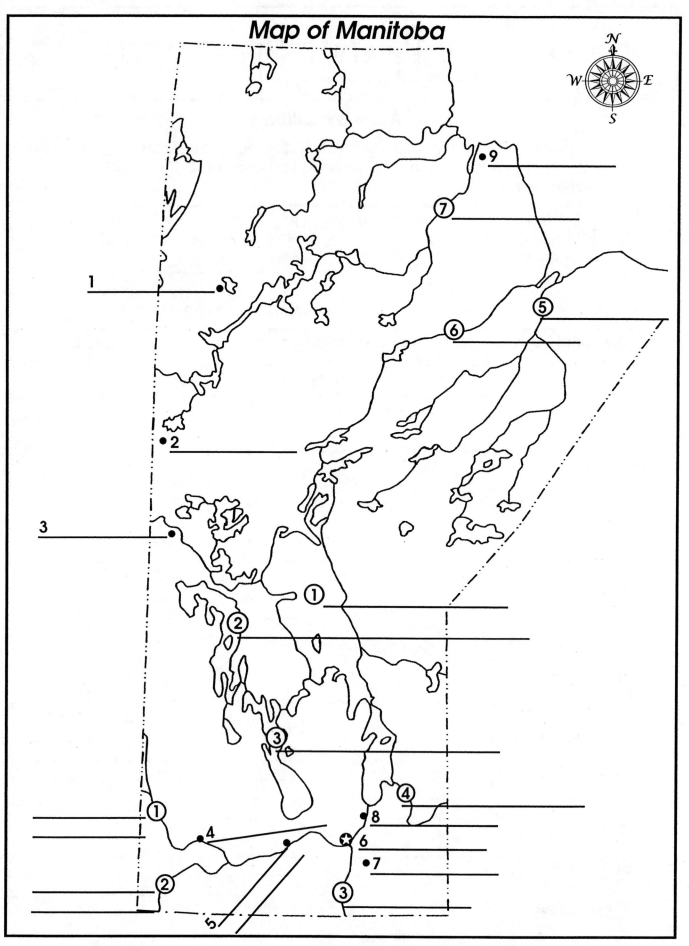

Map of Saskatchewan

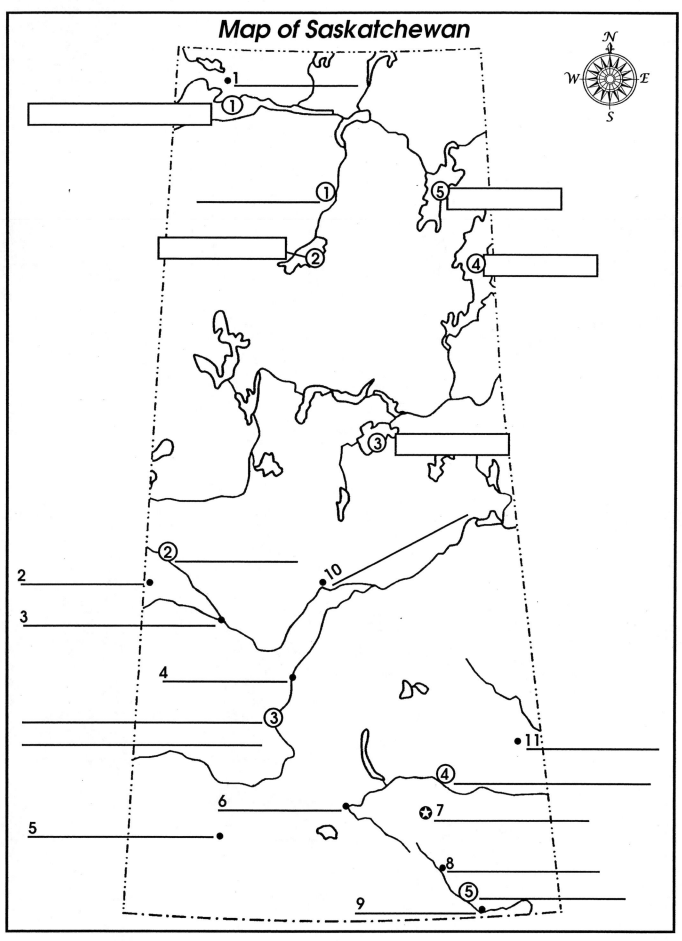

Map of Alberta

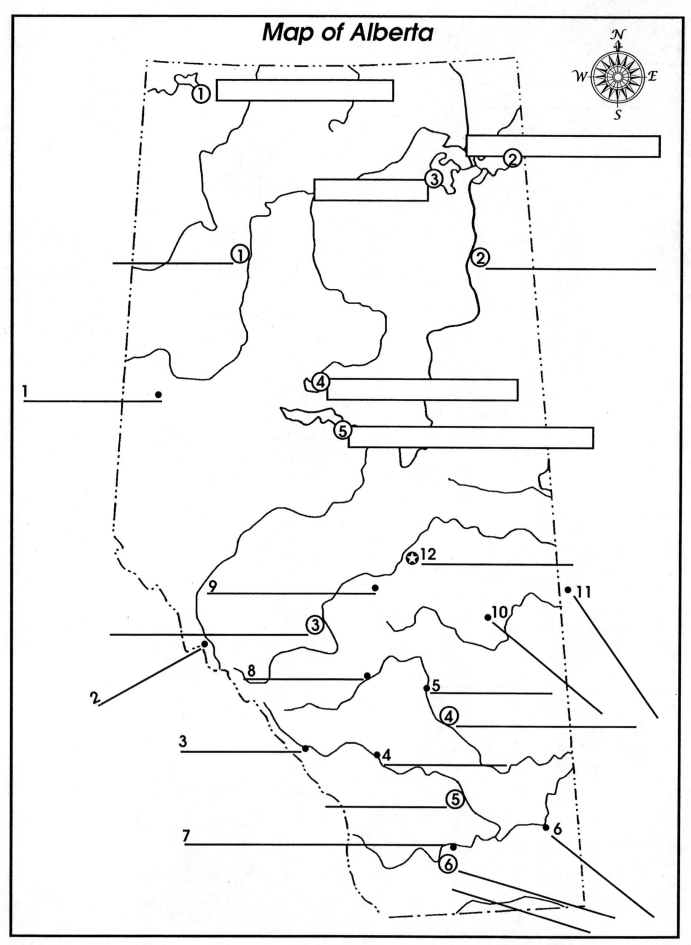

Canada's most western province or Pacific Province is British Columbia. It is the third largest province in land area: 947 800 square kilometres. This province's main physical region is called the North American Cordillera which stretches along the west coast of North America from the tip of Alaska to the southern part of Central America.

In British Columbia are found six main land regions. They are the Insular Mountains, the Lower Fraser Valley, the Coast Mountains, the Interior Plateau, the Eastern Mountains (Rocky Mountains) and the Transmontane Plains.

The Insular Mountains are part of a mountain range that lies mostly under the ocean. The higher parts form many of the islands along the British Columbia's coast. Vancouver Island and the Queen Charlotte Islands are the high parts of the submerged mountain range.

The Lower Fraser Valley is a delta region found in the southwestern corner of the mainland. It is the main farming area of the province. Its soils are fertile and its climate is mild.

The Coast Mountains extend north westward from the Lower Fraser Valley into the Yukon Territory. They give British Columbia a high, indented coastline.

The Interior Plain lies east of the Coast Mountains. The Nicola, Okanagan and Thompson Valleys are important farming, fruit growing and cattle grazing areas found on the plain. The northern part of the plateau is heavily forested.

The Eastern Mountains include the Rocky Mountains and other ranges. The Rocky Mountain Trench is a long, narrow valley that runs north and south from Montana (U.S.) to the Yukon Territory. The Koonenay, Columbia, Fraser, Parsnip and Finlay Rivers flow along the trench.

The Transmontane Plains are flat lands and hilly areas that lie in the northeastern corner of the province. The Peace River District is found on these plains.

British Columbia's coastline is 25 725 kilometres long. Many islands and high mountains are found along the coast. Narrow inlets extend far inland. The narrow waterway between the many islands and coast, called the Inside Passageway, provides a safe waterway for ships to travel.

Many lakes and rivers are found throughout British Columbia. Many chief rivers drain into the Pacific Ocean.

BRITISH COLUMBIA

More than half of the people in British Columbia live in the Vancouver-Victoria region in the southwestern corner of the province. Its population is 3 907 738 (2001 census). Vancouver is its largest city and Canada's busiest port. Other large cities are Surrey, Burnaby, Richmond, Saanich and Delta. Victoria is its capital city and is located on the eastern tip of Vancouver Island. Ferries carry goods and passengers between Vancouver Island and the mainland.

The climate in British Columbia is mild and wet all year along the coast. Winter is rainy with temperatures usually above freezing. Summer is warm with less rain. Interior valleys experience a drier climate. The mountains prevent much of the moist Pacific air from blowing inland. Summers in the interior valleys are warm; winters are cold and snow covers the ground. Skies are usually clear and blue. Northern interior areas are also dry but colder during the winter. On the mountains it is always cold and the highest mountains are always snow-capped all year.

Forests and minerals are British Columbia's main natural resources. The forests found along the coast contain evergreen trees that grow very large such as the Douglas fir and red cedar. The interior valleys are covered in forests as well but the trees are smaller. Logging and mining are important industries in British Columbia. Minerals such as copper, coal, zinc and lead are mined. Many wood and paper products are manufactured in British Columbia as well as food and beverage processing. British Columbia's fishing industry is the largest in Canada. Salmon is the main seafood caught. Farming is mainly done in the southern areas such as the Fraser Valley and the Okanagan Valley. Tourism plays an important role in British Columbia's economy. People from all over the world come to view the beautiful scenery and to visit the many tourist attractions.

Symbols of British Columbia

BRITISH COLUMBIA

Location

A) Complete each sentence with the correct ending. Write the ending on the line.

- Alberta
- the United States
- highly indented
- its west coast
- part of the state of Alaska
- the Northwest Territories and the Yukon
- most westerly province

1. British Columbia is Canada's _____ .
2. British Columbia is bounded on the east by _____ .
3. It is bounded on the north by _____
   _____ .
4. It is bounded on the south by _____ .
5. The Pacific Ocean washes _____ .
6. The western coast of British Columbia is _____ .
7. A long part of the western coast is _____ .

Surface

1. In which physical region of Canada is British Columbia found?
   _____

2. What ocean is to the west of British Columbia? _____

3. Use one word to describe British Columbia's coastline. _____

4. Which mountain range forms the backbone of British Columbia?
   _____

5. Name two other mountain ranges found in Alberta. _____
   _____

6. What large islands are part of a submerged mountain range in British Columbia?
   _____

7. Name three important passes located in the Rocky Mountains.
   _____
   _____

8. Where is the interior plateau?
   _____
   _____

Climate

British Columbia's climate is quite _____. Areas that are separated by _____ or a _____ often experience _____ climates. The west coast of _____ _____ receives over 250 centimetres of rainfall yearly. The island is _____ and _____ and heavily _____. On the opposite side of Vancouver Island lie the _____ in the Strait of Georgia. These islands lie in a _____ and do not receive as much rainfall, so the climate is _____ and _____.

The _____ of the province is _____ and _____ than along the coast in the _____ and _____ in the _____.

_____ winds from the Pacific Ocean _____ British Columbia's coast in the winter and _____ it in summer. _____ ocean winds bring much rain to the coastal regions especially in the _____ and _____. If the winds rise over the _____, their moisture turns into _____ and falls on the western slopes. Land east of the mountains remains _____.

Areas to the north have _____, _____ winters; however, their summers are _____ and the growing period is long enough to grow grain and other crops.

Bristish Columbia's Waterways

British Columbia's landscape is made up of thousands of lakes, rivers and streams. Most of the large lakes such as the Okanagan Lake in the south and the Babine Lake in the north are long and narrow. The lakes lie in valleys formed by the mountains and plateaus.

The Okanagan and the Shuswap are lakes found in the south and are used by tourists and campers. Lake Williston and Lake Nechako are reservoirs created by damming rivers for hydro-electricity. They are the biggest man-made lakes in the province. The largest natural lake is Babine Lake.

British Columbia's rivers flow in a north-south direction for most of their route following the valleys between the mountain ranges. The main rivers of British Columbia drain into the Pacific Ocean. They are the Fraser, Skeena and the Stikine, which are also important salmon rivers. The Fraser River is British Columbia's major river because it drains about one-quarter of the total area of the province. It begins as a tiny trickle in the Rockies gathering silt and debris along its way while growing into a huge waterway, 1 280 kilometres in length. This massive river has cut a deep, spectacular canyon into the Interior Plateau. At a spot called Hell's Gate, the river rushes through canyon walls 1 000 metres high.

BRITISH COLUMBIA

The Nechako, Quesnel, Chilcotin and Thompson Rivers flow into the Fraser. The Laird and Peace Rivers flow eastward and are part of the Mackenzie River System which empties into the Arctic Ocean. The Columbia River, the second longest river in North America, is 1 995 kilometres long and it drains areas in Canada and the United States. Its water is used for generating hydro-electric power and for irrigation. The Kootenay River is the chief tributary of the Columbia River in British Columbia.

Many waterfalls are found in the mountains of British Columbia. The Della Falls on Vancouver Island is 440 metres high. Near the Bella Coola River in the Coast Mountains is Hulen Falls that is 274 metres high. In the Yoho Valley of the Rockies is the Takakkaw Falls that stands 254 metres high.

1. Read the information on "British Columbia's Waterways".

2. Write true or false after the following statements.
   a) The rivers of British Columbia are different from those of the other provinces in that they are more turbulent and flow faster. _____
   b) The Fraser Is the longest river in Canada. _____
   c) The Columbia River is entirely in British Columbia. _____
   d) Salmon are caught in the Fraser River. _____
   e) The Skeena River empties into the Pacific Ocean. _____
   f) The Okanagan is the largest, natural lake in British Columbia. _____
   g) The Fraser River is the longest river in British Columbia. _____
   h) Lake Williston and Lake Nechako are large, man-made lakes. _____
   i) The Takakkaw Falls in the Yoho Valley is the highest falls in British Columbia. _____
   j) The Laird River and the Peace River flow into the Columbia River. _____

3. On the accompanying map locate and label the following waterways.

Rivers
Stikine River, Laird River, Nass River, Skeena River, Thompson River, Fraser River, Columbia River, Okanagan River, Chilcotin River

Lakes
Williston Lake, Babine Lake, Shuswap Lake, Okanagan Lake, Kootenay Lake, Quesnel Lake

Other
Pacific Ocean, Strait of Georgia, Queen Charlotte Strait, Juan de Fuca Strait, Hecate Strait, Queen Charlotte Islands, Vancouver Island

Industries
Forestry

_____ of people work at jobs in the forest industry and the province _____ many forest products. The trees that are _____ are used to make _____, _____ and _____ products, _____ and _____. Workers are _____, biologists, _____, paper mill workers and tree _____.

SSJ1-38

The forests are very _____ to all British Columbians. The forests must be _____ or _____ as they are cut. The dwindling supply of trees has caused _____ between forest companies and other groups in the province.

Some groups feel _____ should not be permitted in certain places. Groups are against certain logging methods such as _____ which is the _____ of large areas of forests at one time. These methods may cause damage to the environment. First Nation groups want their _____ settled. _____ _____ want to protect their jobs and communities. _____ do not want unsightly clear cuts where tourism is high. Pulp and paper _____ want a reliable source of wood for their businesses. _____ want to preserve the old-growth forests and watersheds. In order to resolve these various disputes the government has established a _____ to work with the various groups to protect the _____ and the _____.

Mining

The _____ in the Western Cordillera contain a wide variety of valuable minerals. _____, _____, asbestos, _____, _____, silver, _____, lead and molybdenum are minerals mined in British Columbia. The mining industry employs workers such as _____, _____, engineers, heavy equipment workers, and many others.

The mine at _____ produces _____. The smelter at _____ processes aluminum. In the Peace River area _____ is produced. _____ is mined in the southeast corner of the province. Silver, lead and zinc are extracted in the _____ _____ area. Copper is the most _____ mineral mined.

Mining is not always a _____ industry as the need for certain minerals changes. A mining town can suddenly _____ when the material mined is no longer in demand. This has happened in British Columbia when a _____ depends on the mine as the _____ employer.

Energy

There is an abundance of _____ _____ found in British Columbia. There are _____ coalfields that produce coal which is exported to the _____ countries.

_____ and _____ are piped down the _____ from the Peace River district to Vancouver and the state of Washington. Other pipelines service other parts of the province.

_____ is made by harnessing the power of four of British Columbia's great rivers: the _____, the _____, the _____ and the _____. The _____ built on these rivers supply _____ power to British Columbia.

BRITISH COLUMBIA

Fishing

Fishing in British Columbia is big _____ . This industry has supported people for _____ of years. The fishing and acquaculture industries harvest more than _____ species of _____ and _____ animals. Along the coast many _____ plants are located as well as numerous _____ farms that raise _____ or _____. Thousands of boats are used in the fishing _____.

People employed in the fishing industry are fishing boat _____, marine _____, processing-plant _____ and fish _____. Two important fishing centres are _____ in the north and _____ in the south.

British Columbia's waters are fished for salmon such as _____, _____, _____, _____ and _____. Salmon is _____ prized around the world whether it is _____, _____ or _____. It makes up more than _____ of the province's ocean _____.

_____ is also fished for its _____ or _____. Tonnes of herring are caught each _____. The roe is removed from the mature _____ fish and exported to _____. The mass of eggs or roe is a traditional _____ in Japan. The _____ of the herrings are processed for _____ and _____.

The fishing industry in British Columbia has many groups concerned about the _____ fish population. It is felt this situation has been caused by _____ fishers, _____ fishers and _____ fishers.

Tourism

British Columbia's spectacular _____ and _____ climate of the southern coast attracts visitors the year round. _____ and _____ are popular cities filled with exciting tourist attractions. The _____ and their resorts attract downhill skiers and cross-country skiers in the _____. In the summer _____, tennis players, hikers and _____ enjoy the area. The wide variety of _____ attracts many tourists.

British Columbia's Cities

1. _____ is British Columbia's _____ city and the _____ port in Canada. Its _____ _____ in Burrard Inlet never _____ and allows ships to use it _____. The port handles nearly all of Canada's trade with _____ and other _____ countries. Vancouver is often called _____ _____ .

BRITISH COLUMBIA

Vancouver has a _____ setting as it is located near the _____ and the _____. Its _____ is mild as the city is protected by the _____ and it receives _____ blowing in from the Pacific Ocean. Its _____ and _____ make it a very inviting place to live. Its thriving _____, _____ and _____ communities make it a strong _____ city.

Victoria

Victoria is the _____ _____ of British Columbia. It is located at the _____ tip of _____ _____. It is called _____ _____ due to the _____ climate that allows flowers to bloom _____. _____ _____, located near Victoria, is one of Canada's most _____ gardens. Many of Victoria's buildings are _____ and _____ and remind tourists of buildings in England. The _____ Hotel is an outstanding, elegant, tourist attraction. _____ can be found in the Royal British Columbia Museum and Thunderbird Park.

Vancouver Island Butchart Gardens

Totem Poles, Victoria

2. On the map of British Columbia, locate and name the following cities. The capital city is marked with a star inside a circle.

Vancouver	**New Westminister**	**Victoria**	**Powell River**	**Duncan**
Nanaimo	**Prince Rupert**	**Kamloops**	**Port Alberni**	**Kitimat**
Penticton	**Prince George**	**Kelowna**	**Dawson Creek**	

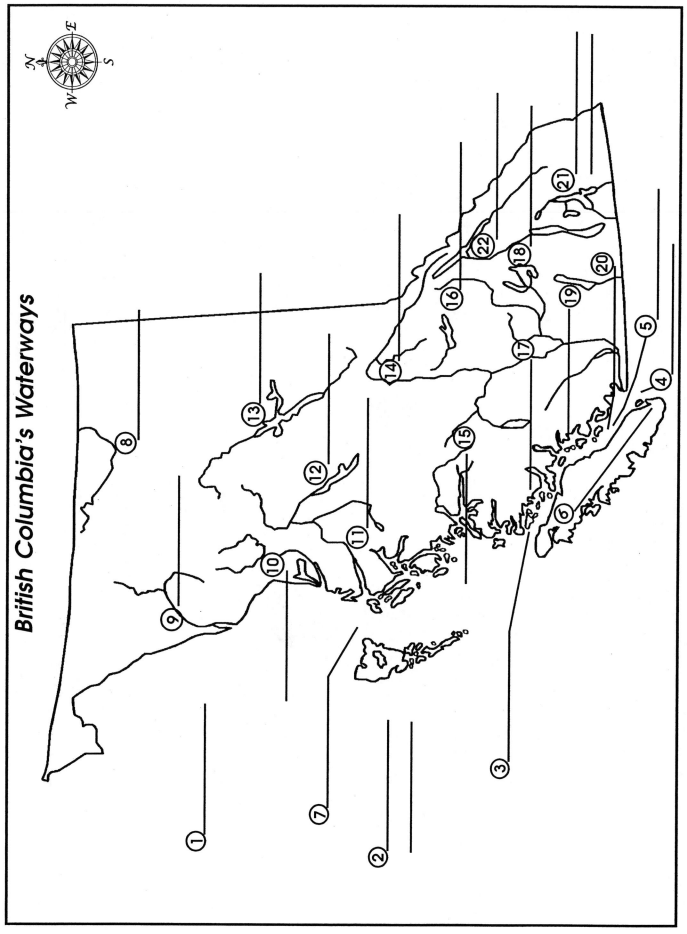

British Columbia's Waterways

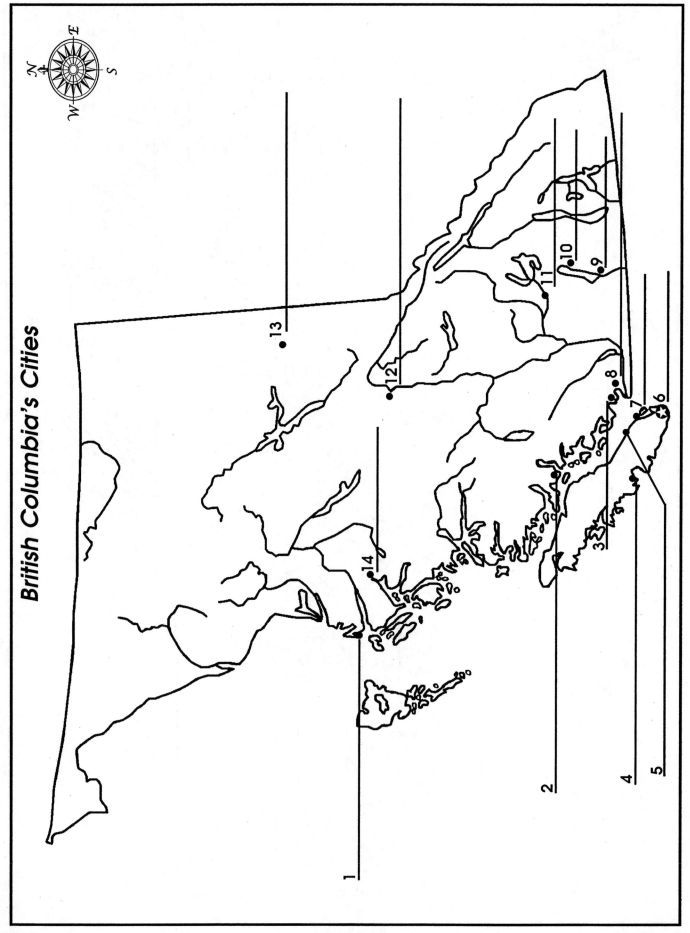

British Columbia's Cities

The territories make up more than one third of Canada's land mass. They are located in the northernmost part of Canada. There are three territories: the Yukon Territory, the Northwest Territories and Nunavut.

The Yukon

The Yukon is a pie-shaped wedge located in the northwestern corner of Canada. It is squeezed between the Northwest Territories on the east, Alaska on the west and British Columbia to the south, while the icy waters of the Beaufort Sea form the Yukon's northern coastline.

Many long chains of rugged mountains divided by plateaus and deep valleys are found throughout the territory. These land forms are a part of the Cordillera, a belt of mountainous terrain, that stretches along the entire edge of North and South America. Many glaciers and ice fields are found in the mountains. The mighty Yukon River, the second longest river in Canada, flows through this territory. It is fed by other large rivers such as the Porcupine, the Klondike and the Pelly. In the northernmost areas along the Arctic Coast, the ground remains frozen year round, and is called permafrost.

The Yukon's climate is long and cold during the winter months and some areas near the Arctic Circle do not receive any sunshine. Winter lasts from September to June. In the summer the opposite occurs. From the end of May until the middle of July the sun never sets. Yukon summers are warm, and temperature can vary between 10°C to 27°C. Very little rain or snow falls in the Yukon and the air is quite dry.

The population of the Yukon in 1999 was 31,305, made up of a variety of ethnic backgrounds. The capital of the Yukon is Whitehorse, which at that time had a population of 22 984.

Gold and other minerals are mined and mining employs about six per cent of the people in the Yukon. Many other people in the Yukon are employed by the government. Some people work as guides to sport fishermen or hunters, or they take people rafting on many of the scenic rivers during the summer. Some farming and ranching is also done. Elk, bison, reindeer and musk oxen are raised for their meat and hides. Many of the Native Peoples create beautiful art pieces for tourists to buy, or they sell them elsewhere.

The Northwest Territories

The Northwest Territories is a large area of land located between the Yukon to the west, Nunavut to the east, the Arctic Ocean to the north and British Columbia, Alberta and Saskatchewan to the south.

The Canadian Shield and the Interior Plains are the two main physical regions in this territory. Most of the Northwest Territories lies above the tree line. The Northwest Territories is filled with majestic mountains, winding rivers, deep valleys, rushing waterfalls and pine forests.

The Mackenzie River is the longest river in Canada and empties into the Arctic Ocean. It flows through the Mackenzie Valley where most of the people in the territory live. Yellowknife is the capital city and is found in the Mackenzie Valley as well. It is here where many people live. The population in the Northwest Territories is approximately 58 000. The people are from a variety of ethnic backgrounds.

The land near the Arctic Ocean is rocky and treeless tundra. The permanently frozen ground of the tundra is called permafrost.

The Northwest Territories experiences a dry climate. It receives very little snow or rain throughout the year. Winters are extremely cold with temperatures about -32° C. Temperatures in the Mackenzie Valley can be warmer. In the summer, temperatures may hover around 21° C.

The people who live in the Territories must be very versatile as the work is seasonal. Many Native People hunt and fish for food and trap animals for their furs. Some take tourists on guided tours, camping trips and fishing expeditions throughout the land. Handicrafts are made to sell to the tourists and they are also sold to other markets. Some mining of gold is done at Yellowknife. Oil is produced at Norman Wells. Many people are employed by the government and perform important service jobs.

Nunavut

Nunavut is a newly formed territory that has been carved out of the Northwest Territories. On April 1, 1999 it was officially declared a Canadian territory with its own government and judicial court. Its name means "our land" in Inuktituk.

Nunavut is located east of the Northwest Territories and north of Manitoba. It has a greater land area than any other province or territory and the longest coast line in Canada. Nunavut is shaped something like an "inukshuk" or pile of stones stacked to look like a human. Most of Nunavut is made up of the Canadian Shield. It is divided into two main land regions: the Arctic Mainland and the Arctic Islands. Most of the land is rocky, swampy, or permafrost.

The communities are small, few in number and spread far apart. Large communities are Iqaluit, Rankin Inlet and Cambridge Bay. Iqaluit is the capital city of this new territory. The total population of Nunavut is approximately 22 000. Mainly Inuit live in this territory.

Nunavut has the coldest weather in Canada. The average temperature is 9^0 C. In the winter the temperature can dip to a chilling -30^0 C. Freezing winds, icy blizzards and blowing snow make the winters seem even colder. During the summer, places closest to the North Pole in Nunavut have sunlight all day and night as the earth is tilted towards the sun. In the winter, it is the opposite and there is no sunlight or light of any kind for days. Nunavut receives very little snow or rain.

Nunavut does not have any highways or roads connecting the communities. The people must travel by air, boat or an all-terrain vehicle. In the winter they use snowmobiles or dog sleds.

Inuit fill a variety of positions within the workforce of Nunavut. They perform an assortment of jobs, which can include guides to tourists, construction workers and artisans. Inuit are being trained in many service jobs, and are the teachers, nurses, doctors, electricians, etc. of this territory. The Inuit elders continue teaching children the traditional ways and values of the Inuit society.

Symbols of the Yukon Territory

Symbols of The Northwest Territories

Symbols of The Nunavut

THE TERRITORIES

Location

The Yukon Territory

The Yukon Territory is located in the extreme _____ part of Canada. It is _____ in shape. To the west it borders the state of _____ and to the east it borders the _____. The Yukon's southern border is the province of _____ and to the north it borders the salt waters of the _____.

The Northwest Territories

The Northwest Territories is located in the _____ of Canada's northern territories. To the west it borders the _____ and to the east it borders _____. To the north it borders the _____ and to the south it borders the provinces of _____, _____, and _____.

Nunavut Territory

Nunavut is a new territory carved out of the _____ for the _____ people. On the _____ it borders the Northwest Territories and to the east across Baffin Bay and Davis Strait lies the country of _____. To the south it borders _____ and to the north the _____.

Surface

The Yukon Territory

The Yukon Territory is an area filled with _____, _____ and _____ separated by _____. The Yukon is divided into four main regions. They are the _____, the _____, the _____ and the _____. The _____ Range and the _____ Mountains cover the southwestern corner of the Yukon. Some of the _____ peaks in North America are found in these mountains. _____, a massive mountain, is found in the Saint Elias Range and it is the _____ mountain in _____ and the second highest in _____. It is _____ metres high. _____ and permanent _____ are also found in the Saint Elias Mountains.

The Northwest Territories

The Northwest Territories is one of North America's last _____ regions. It is filled with majestic _____, deep _____, pine _____ and some _____ islands. It has _____ main physical regions.

         SSJ1-38

THE TERRITORIES

They are the _____, the _____ and the _____. The Northwest Territories is covered mainly by the _____ which is a huge _____ of solid _____ that is two to four billion years old. This bedrock is the storage place for many of Canada's _____.

Nunavut

Nunavut has two-thirds of Canada's _____. It is _____ than any other territory or province in Canada. Its coastline is stretched around many islands, bays, channels and inlets. Nunavut is located "_____", a region of the world where _____. Much of this territory rests on the hard rock called the _____ _____.

Territorial Climates

The Yukon Territory

The Yukon Territory is located in the _____ climate zone. Its temperatures can range from _____ or colder to _____ or warmer. Winters are _____ and _____. Lakes and rivers begin to _____ by early October. By the _____ of _____ some places receive _____ daylight while other places may receive _____ to _____ hours of light.

The Yukon Territory has a _____ climate and receives _____ snowfalls. There is so little _____ that the main roads do not get _____.

Yukon summers are _____ but _____. Temperatures usually reach the mid-twenties. The middle of summer falls on June 21 which is the _____ day of the season and year. Places like Old Crow experience _____ of sun, Dawson City receives _____ and Whitehorse and Watson get _____. Throughout the territory the _____ lasts almost to _____. The Yukon is often referred to as the "_____" for this reason.

The Northwest Territories

The Northwest Territories is _____ covered with _____ and _____ all year long. It receives _____ snow than many places in _____ Canada. Snow does fall but it gets _____ away by howling _____. It seldom _____ in the Northwest Territories. Some scientists classify it as a _____ because it is so dry.

Summers can be quite _____ and sometimes even _____. Summer temperatures often hover around _____. July temperatures in Fort Smith have been recorded as high as _____.

SSJ1-38

THE TERRITORIES

Winters are very _____ with harsh _____ and are very _____.
Winter in the _____ areas lasts for at least _____ months.

In the spring, snow and ice still cover the ground but the people _____
the arrival of spring. It is still cold but the sunlight is _____ and appears
_____. The days are _____. Summer is _____ but
the plants grow _____ due to the _____ _____ of
daylight.

Nunavut

Nunavut has the _____ weather in Canada. Winter lasts about
_____ months and the average temperature is _____. During this season
_____, _____ and _____ _____
are experienced which make the winter appear even _____.

In the summer Nunavut can get quite _____. Temperatures have been
recorded as high as _____ in Coppermine, one of Nunavut's coastal communities.

Nunavut is also considered the "Land of the Midnight Sun". During the
_____, the North Pole tilts _____ the sun. Hence the areas of Nunavut
that are _____ to the North Pole have summer days of almost _____
_____ even at _____. In the winter it is the _____. During
this season the North Pole tilts _____ from the sun and the _____ areas
of Nunavut experience _____ _____.

Industries

The Yukon Territory

The Canadian Government heavily subsidizes the Yukon Territory due to its remoteness
and small population. Without this help the Yukon could not keep up to its present standard.

Mining

Mining has been the _____ of the Yukon's economy ever since _____
was discovered in the _____ a hundred years ago. _____ mining
accounts for _____ per cent of the Yukon's mineral production. _____ and
_____ are now the territory's most important minerals. Many of the large mines have
closed down because the _____ was _____ or because the
_____ metal prices were too _____ to carry on with mining operations.

THE TERRITORIES

Tourism

Tourism is the Yukon's _____ largest industry. Travellers come from all over the world to view its _____ beauty and learn its _____. Tourists come to participate in wilderness _____, _____ and river _____. Tourism _____ almost a _____ of the territory's non-government workforce.

The Government

The _____ employs the _____ number of people in the territory. They perform a wide range of jobs for the _____, _____ and _____ governments.

The Fur Trade

Fur _____ and _____ is the Yukon's oldest industry. It dates back in time to when the _____ first began to explore the territory. Trapping today does provide a living for _____ Yukoners but it is an _____ occupation. Fur prices often _____ and the _____ for fur coats and fur clothing has _____ in recent years. _____, _____, _____, _____ and _____ are the popular animals that are trapped for their furs.

Forestry

Trees grow very _____ in the Yukon and take _____ years to mature. _____ started by _____ strikes destroy millions of hectares of trees every year. Forestry is _____ an important industry in the Yukon. There are _____ _____ mills near _____ in southeastern Yukon. Several small sawmills operate near _____.

Farming

Farming areas are limited in the Yukon due to _____ soil, low _____ and _____. In good areas where farming is successful the _____ hours of _____ help the plants to grow _____.

Although farming is not an _____ industry there are a number of _____ farming operations. Near Dawson, where the soil has been made fertile by the flooding of rivers, _____ and certain _____ grow successfully. In the _____ area there are a small number of family-run _____ farms. They produce products such as _____, _____, _____, _____, rabbits, _____, sheep, _____, fish and _____. A farm on the _____ River successfully raises _____ and _____.

THE TERRITORIES

Fishing

Fishing is more _____ to the Yukon economy than farming. At Dawson, _____ and _____ salmon are caught in the rivers and then processed. These fish are _____ to Germany, Japan and other countries. _____ is plentiful and sold commercially. _____, a northern delicacy, is sold to restaurants all over the world. _____ fishing brings in many _____ to the Yukon. _____ from all over the world love to fish in the Yukon's sparkling, cold, clear _____ found in its lakes and streams.

The Northwest Territories

Mining

The Northwest Territories is known to have almost every _____ that has been discovered. These minerals will play an _____ role in the _____ of the Northwest Territories. At the present time it is very _____ to _____ the minerals and to _____ them to other countries. The _____ has very ambitious plans for overcoming these obstacles. Mining is the _____ _____ industry and brings in _____ _____ than any other industry.

Oil and Gas

In the Northwest Territories _____ areas seem rich in _____, while _____ areas are richer in _____. There are three _____ oil and gas fields in the Northwest Territories. They are located at _____ in the Arctic Islands, _____ near Fort Laird and _____ on the Mackenzie River. The Norman Wells oil field has been the most successful. Six _____ were constructed in the Mackenzie River in 1982 and a _____ from Norman Wells to Zama, Alberta was built in 1985 to link up with other pipelines.

Trapping and Hunting

The fur trade is the _____ industry in the Northwest Territories and once was the _____. The _____ and people who are _____ for their fur have weakened this industry. The animals mainly caught are _____, _____ and _____ fox, _____, _____, _____, _____, _____ and _____.

 SSJ1-38

Many animals such as _____, _____, _____, _____, _____ and various birds such as _____, _____, _____ and _____ are hunted and eaten by small communities. Wild game is _____ and _____ to other places.

_____ is an important industry as _____ come from around the world to hunt _____ such as polar bear, musk-ox, caribou, moose and grizzly bear. The _____ is considered the ultimate adventure for a hunter. Each hunter may pay up to _____ for a hunt. The _____ can earn _____ money by providing the service.

Fishing

The people in the Northwest Territories have fished the _____ and _____ for food for many years. Today fishing is also a _____ industry. Many _____ come to fish for _____ and are asked to _____ any fish they catch. This helps to protect the _____ of fish. Fishing _____ are open from June to September. _____ and _____ are popular fishing spots. Great Slave Lake also has a _____ whitefish fishery.

Forestry

Forestry is _____ a big industry in the Northwest Territories because it is _____ to areas south of the _____. There is a large area of _____ forest but there are very few _____. The forestry industry has not grown due to the _____ of roads, and the _____ of money and _____ people.

Farming

The Northwest Territories does have some _____, but they are not like the ones we see in the rest of Canada. Most of the farms are found near _____. Here you will find a _____ farm, an _____ production farm, a _____ ranch, a _____ ranch and a large _____. Near _____ there is more market gardening. _____ has a small cattle ranch and near _____ a herd of _____ provides _____ and _____ for a small market.

_____ gardening, _____ and local _____ gardens help to provide fresh vegetables.

THE TERRITORIES

Nunavut's Industries

Nunavut is very _____ and _____ is either _____ or _____ therefore very few _____ have developed in the territory. The _____ of Nunavut is shaped by many factors which include climate, lifestyle and resources.

The Inuit's Lifestyle

Inuit work at a _____ of jobs. Some of the jobs they have are as _____ and _____. These jobs are seasonal. The Inuit are well known _____, making _____, _____ and _____ specific to the Inuit way of life. This art is sold in local communities, as well as exported and sold in shops across North America.

Government Jobs

The Inuit have a variety of positions, some of these in the service sector running their _____. They are the _____, _____, electricians, and teachers of the future. Inuit are striving to be at the cutting edge of developing their territory.

Tourism

Tourism is the _____ growing part of the territory's economy. The Inuit _____ at jobs as tour guides, hotel clerks and cooks. Many work as _____. An outfitter _____ outdoor equipment such as _____ and _____ to visitors who come to _____ Nunavut's _____ wilderness.

Hunting and fishing _____ take tourists to good fishing areas. Some help tourists _____ the wild rivers or _____ amongst the Arctic Islands. Because of their extensive knowledge of the land, Inuit guides take tourists on _____ trips across the tundra or help them _____ mountains and glaciers.

Construction

Communities in Nunavut are _____ _____. The construction business is very _____. New buildings such as _____, _____, _____ centres and _____ are being constructed.

Mining

Nunavut has _____ _____ of minerals. Miners dig for _____ and _____ at the Polaris Mine on _____ or at the Nanisivik mine near _____. The _____ on _____ is the world's northermost gold mine. It is one of Canada's top five _____ producers. _____ and _____ has also been located in Nunavut. There is one small oil field in production called _____ on _____.

Manufacturing

There are very few _____ in Nunavut. Most workers work at _____ food. Raw _____ and _____ are cut up and packaged. Nunavut plans to _____ more factories to _____ more jobs.

The Yukon's Cities and Towns

1. _____ is the capital city of the Yukon Territory. It lies on the _____bank of the _____ River. Large _____ homes can be seen standing with older _____, still in use on the streets. One major tourist attraction is the two-and-three-storey _____. Tourists love to tour the _____, the largest and last of the _____ that travelled the Yukon River.

2. _____ is famous for its Klondike Gold Rush days. It lies at the junction of the _____ and the _____ Rivers. Every year tourists come to wander the town's _____ streets and wooden _____ and stop at _____ log cabin to hear actors reading his poetry. Dawson City's streets are lined with brightly painted _____, _____ and _____ that look the same as they did during the gold rush.

3. On a map of the Yukon locate and label the important centres listed below. The capital city is located at the star inside a circle.

Teslin	**Watson Lake**	**Whitehorse**	**Dawson City**	**Faro**
Old Crow	**Haines Junction**	**Carcross**	**Carmacks**	

The Northwest Territories' Cities and Towns

1. _____ is the capital city of the Northwest Territories. It is located on the north shore of _____. Yellowknife is considered the _____ to the entire territory. Yellowknife's _____ have a mixture of large _____, _____ houses, _____ shacks and _____ huts which were _____ homes left by the early _____. Tourists enjoy driving the _____, sailing on _____ or cruising the _____.

2. _____ is known as the Garden Capital of the North. The _____ largest _____ park in the world is found near Fort Smith. It is called _____. _____ come here to travel through the historic _____ and _____ _____ on the Slave River.

3. _____ is the _____ Canadian Community _____ of the Arctic Circle. It was the first _____ town built by the government to replace _____ which appeared to be sinking into the _____.

4. On a map of the Northwest Territories, mark on the following cities and towns. The capital city is marked with a star inside a circle.

Tuktoyaktuk	**Inuvik**	**Yellowknife**	**Fort Simpson**	**Fort Smith**
Fort Resolution	**Rae**	**Fort Norman**	**Hay River**	**Pine Point**
Norman Wells	**Wrigley**	**Fort Laird**	**Deline**	

The Cities and Towns of Nunavut

1. Many of the communities in Nunavut are _____, _____ in number and _____ from one another. There are approximately _____ people living in Nunavut. The people are scattered about throughout the territory in 28 _____ communities. _____ is the _____ community with 3 552 residents. It is the _____ _____ of Nunavut and is located on _____ Island.

   Every year there is a spring celebration called _____ held in Iqaluit. In _____ there is Tunooniq Theatre where actors portray both the _____ and _____ Inuit ways.

   In Nunavut the ground is _____ frozen; therefore, all the _____ are constructed to sit _____ above ground. Even the _____ carrying _____, and _____ must be _____ ground.

2. Using a map of Nunavut locate and mark the following communities.

Baker Lake	**Cape Dorset**	**Cambridge Bay**	**Coppermine**
Arviat	**Pond Inlet**	**Rankin Inlet**	**Repulse Bay**
Iqaliut	**Pangnirtung**	**Chesterfield Inlet**	**Gjoa Haven**
Resolute	**Whale Cove**	**Alert**	

Cities and Towns of the Yukon Territory

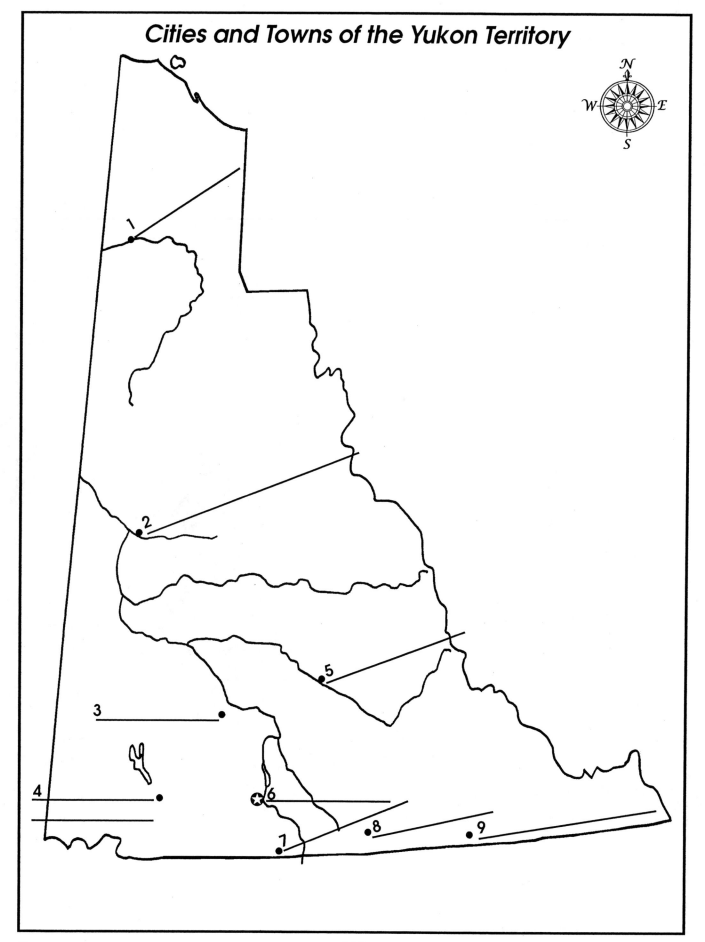

Cities and Towns of the Northwest Territories

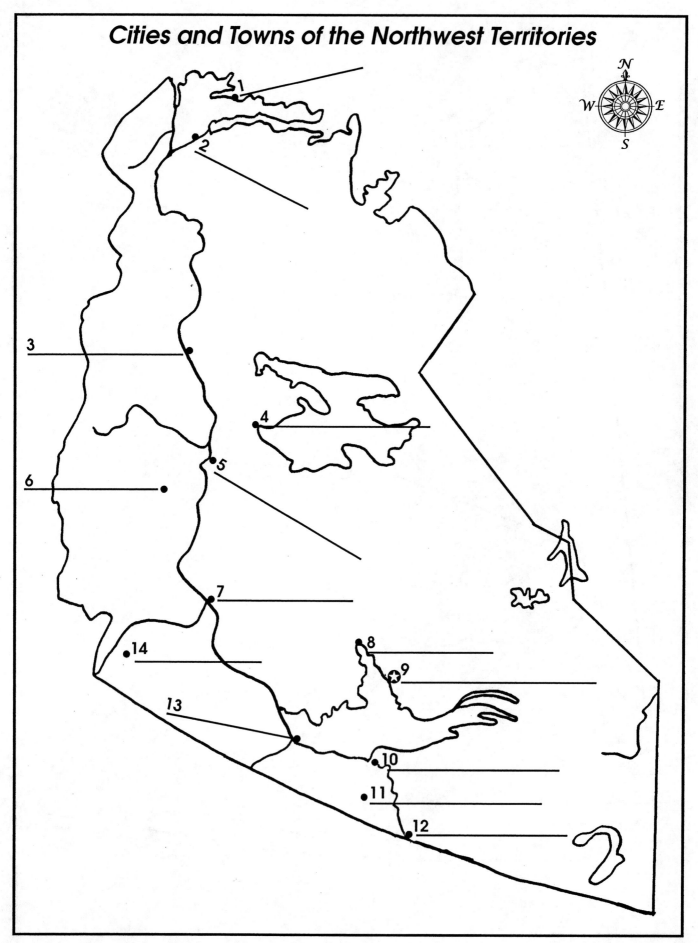

SSJ1-38

Map of Nunavut

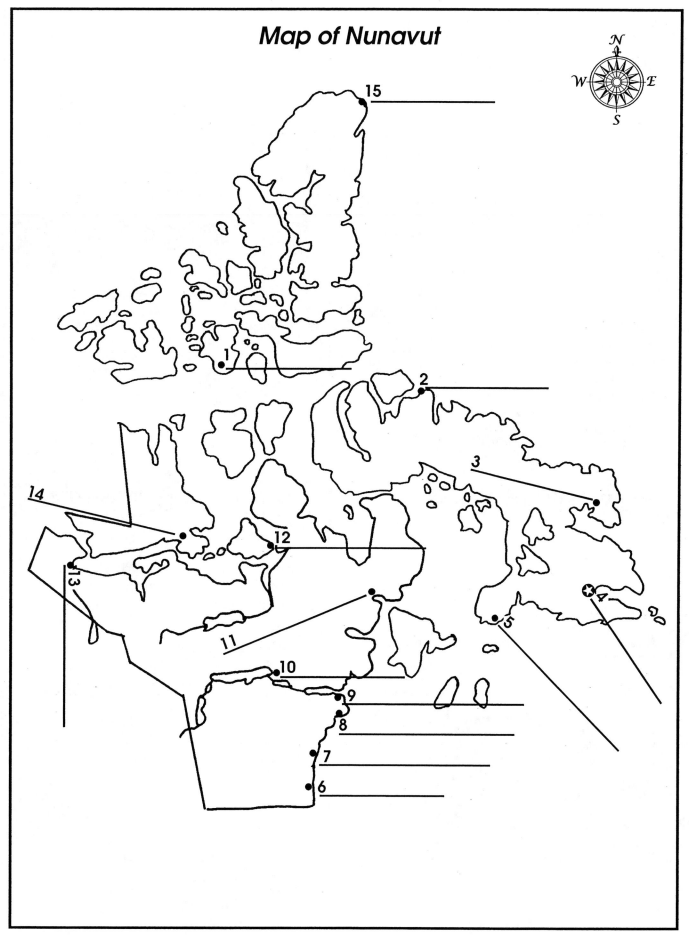

Answer Key

Worksheet #1: Where is Canada? *(page 13)*

second; northern; North America; United States; Mexico; 9 970 610; Russia; A continent is one of the seven dry land masses on the earth; an ocean is a great body of salt water – oceans cover three quarters of the earth's surface; Africa; Asia; Antarctica; Australia; Europe; North America; South America; Arctic Ocean; Atlantic Ocean; Pacific Ocean, Indian Ocean

Worksheet #2: Canada's Borders *(page 14)*

Map: 1. Arctic Ocean   2. Alaska   3. Pacific Ocean   4. Hudson Bay   5. Atlantic Ocean
6. The United States

1. A border is the side or edge or boundary of anything. It can be a line which separates one country, state or province from another. It can be a coastline.
2. Pacific Ocean; Alaska
3. Atlantic Ocean
4. Arctic Ocean; Hudson Bay
5. United States
6. 13   7. No   8. 11   9. 2

Worksheet #3: Canada's Provinces and Territories *(page 15)*

1. ten; territories
2. Alberta; British Columbia; Manitoba; New Brunswick; Newfoundland and Labrador; Northwest Territories; Nova Scotia; Nunavut; Ontario; Prince Edward Island; Québec; Saskatchewan; Yukon Territory
3. Prince Edward Island
4. Nova Scotia, Newfoundland and Labrador, New Brunswick, Prince Edward Island
5. Manitoba, Saskatchewan, Alberta
6. Yukon Territory, Northwest Territories, Nunavut

Worksheet #4: Border Riddles *(page 16)*

1. British Columbia
2. Nova Scotia
3. Ontario
4. Nunavut
5. New Brunswick
6. The Northwest Territories
7. Alberta
8. Manitoba
9. The Yukon Territory
10. Prince Edward Island
11. Saskatchewan
12. Québec
13. Newfoundland and Labrador

Worksheet #5: Canadian Province/Territory and Capital City Search *(page 17)*

```
T M K Q U E B E C C I T Y T U V A N U N P O
E A D S B U W I B J O I F S N G A I N O M A
V N R A Q H C O N T A R I O Z F H B L V C I R
F I Q A L I U T G T J R Q E P X E K D A J O T
X T G L P Z L T V H C T O R O N T O V S U Y C
N O O B Y M A A K U L D W Y M Q W A T C Z I V
C B S E F W G W H I T E H O R S E X B O Z Z I
T A Q R P O V A A I B M Y N F S G R C I T I D
R D U T E H K J N X L N M Z H L E K J D S
H C H A R L O T T E T O W N A R W L Y A P S
I G F V E U J T K D S R L E O B X P Z Q M Q
P Y U K O N D X F B Z T A W I N N I P E G R
O E U Q T A W E C Y H H I F O Y E N A A N E
S L V Q V W U G V T J W K O L O W M G N F D
R L P K R E U J H W I E X U Z D B C B I E M
W O S T N H R P L M I S Q N E N B R Y W G Z O
Z W I S B C O E N H H T I D V Q U E B E C N
D K A L H T X Q O N G T G L F J N C A R X T
F N M J Y A G C T O T E U A K L S M D U B O
X I T M V K Y R C F D R Q N K Z W T Y N X N
U F K Z L S A N I S R R J D S D I O A C V W
Q E R A O A D M R N P I R T Z G C F H M I N
X Y S B C S E E E N O T K P W X K Q P J O R
W C Z B B C F L D P E O U S F A K K G G S M
W W X T D G K D E H Q R I V Y J I L J L H T
V Y D U A F H B R I T I S H C O L U M B I A
B U E C I E G S F U B E E C D D F W N I N C
K M Z S Q J R R V L A S Q P V E O G H X J O
T V H P D N A L S I D R A W D E E C N I R P
L I J O G W T F U X M L M K V Z R U Y P B T
N H A L I F A X Z X Y W S T J O H N S A S Q
```

Worksheet #6: Let's Research Canada! *(page 18)*

1. Nunavut
2. Québec
3. Prince Edward Island
4. Edmonton
5. Regina, Victoria
6. British Columbia, Alberta
7. Winnipeg
8. Toronto
9. Trillium
10. Northwest Territories
11. Ontario
12. Québec City
13. New Brunswick
14. Prince Edward Island
15. Nova Scotia
16. Newfoundland and Labrador
17. Charlottetown
18. Fredericton
19. Prince Edward Island
20. British Columbia

Worksheet #7: Physical Regions of Canada
(page 19)
Answers will vary.

Worksheet #8: Inportant Rivers of Canada *(page20)*
1. Ottawa River, St. Maurice River, Saguenay River
2. Albany River, Moose River, Rupert River, Eastmain River
3. Churchill River, Nelson River, Severn River, La Grande River
4. St. Lawrence River
5. Fraser River, Skeena River
6. North Saskatchewan River, South Saskatchewan River
7. Mackenzie River, Peel River, Coppermine River, Back River
8. Yukon River
9, 10, 11. Answers will vary.

Worksheet #9: How long are the rivers in Canada?
(page 21)
1. Mackenzie River - 4 241 km - Arctic Ocean
2. Yukon River - 3185 km - Bering Sea
3. St. Lawrence River - 3 058 km - Atlantic Ocean
4. Columbia River - 2 000 km - Pacific Ocean
5. Peace River - 1 923 km - Lake Athabasca
6. Churchill River - 1 609 km - Hudson Bay
7. Fraser River - 1 370 km - Pacific Ocean
8. Ottawa River - 1 271 km - St. Lawrence River
9. Athabasca River - 1 231 km - Lake Athabasca
10. Laird River - 1 115 km - Mackenzie River

Worksheet #10(a): Rivers and Lakes of Canada
(page 22)
a) Québec   b) Ontario   c) Ontario
d) Ontario   e) Alberta, British Columbia
f) British Columbia
g) Manitoba, Saskatchewan
h) Saskatchewan, Alberta
i) Ontario   j) Québec   k) Ontario, Québec
l) Ontario   m) Alberta, Northwest Territories
n) British Columbia   o) Ontario
p) British Columbia   q) Saskatchewan
r) British Columbia   s) New Brunswick
t) Newfoundland and Labrador

Worksheet #10(b): Rivers and Lakes of Canada
(page 23)
a) Grand Lake, Smallwood Reservoir
b) Lake St. John, Lake Abitibi, Lake Mistassini
c) Lake Simcoe, Lake Ontario, Lake Nipissing, Lake Nipigon, Lake of the Woods, Lake St. Clair, Lake Huron, Lake Erie

d) Lake Winnipeg, Lake of the Woods, Lake Winnipegosis, Reindeer Lake
e) Lake Athabasca, Reindeer Lake
f) Lake Louise, Lake Athabasca
g) Kootenay Lake, Lake Okanagan
h) Grand Lake
i) Lake Gary
j) Great Slave Lake, Great Bear Lake, Lake Aberdeen

Worksheet #11(a): The Population of Canada
(page 24)
second; ten million; 30 million; uninhabited; rugged; severe

Provinces/Territories from the Smallest to the Largest:
Nunavut - 28 100
Yukon Territory - 29 800
Northwest Territories - 40 800
Prince Edward Island - 138 500
Newfoundland and Labrador - 533 700
New Brunswick - 757 000
Nova Scotia - 942 600
Saskatchewan - 1 015 700
Manitoba - 1 150 000
Alberta - 3 064 200
British Columbia - 4 095 900
Québec - 7 410 500
Ontario - 11 874 400

Worksheet 11(b): Reading a Chart *(page 25)*
1. Answers will vary.
2. Answers will vary.
3. Prince Edward Island
4. Ontario
5. Nunavut
6. 2 410 000
7. Northwest Territories
8. Nova Scotia
9. Saskatchewan
10. 5 229 900
11. 4 463 900
12. 395 200
13. No; Prince Edward Island

Worksheet #12(b): Ethnic Population of Canada
(page 26)
1. British
2. Yes
3. British, French, German
4. Portuguese, Black, Jewish
5. No

CANADIAN PROVINCES AND TERRITORIES

Ethnic Populations from largest to smallest:
British, French, German, Italian, Ukranian, Dutch, Aboriginal, Other, Scandinavian, Polish, East and Southeast Asian, Chinese, Black, Jewish, and Portuguese

Worksheet #13(a&b): Population Distribution
(page 28)
2. They live in the southern most areas of each province.
3. Ontario, Québec, British Columbia
4. It is warmer, better land, closer to the United States markets, most cities are there.
5. Very few live in the territories and the northern areas of the provinces.
6. Answers will vary.
7. They have good land for farming and grazing cattle.
8. This is the main water route to the west. Many cities are ports. There are many factories and places to work. The lakes provide good transportation.
9. They are cold areas. You cannot farm or raise animals very well. They are isolated from the rest of the country. Some places do not have roads in or out.
10. Answers will vary.
11. Answers will vary.

Worksheet #14(a): Climatic Regions of Canada
(page 30)
1. Pacific Region
2. Arctic region
3. The Northern Region
4. The Prairie Region
5. Mountain Region
6. Southeastern Region

Worksheet #14(b): Let's Compare Temperatures
(page 32)
1. No   2. - 8 ^{0}C   3. 16 ^{0}C   4. - 23 ^{0}C
5. Resolute
6. Prince Rupert is closer to the ocean. Kamloops is further south and Prince George is in the mountains.
7. Yellowknife   8. Victoria, Moosonee

Worksheet 14(c): Precipitation and Temperature
(page 33)
1. Winnipeg   2. Yellowknife
3. Victoria   4. St. John's
5. Winnipeg   6. St. John's, Halifax

7. St. John's, Halifax, Charlottetown, Fredericton, Québec City, Toronto
8. Whitehorse, Yellowknife

Community Climate:
Answers will vary.

Worksheet #15: Natural Vegetation Regions
(page 35)
1. coniferous, deciduous
2. low shrubs, mosses, lichens
3. British Columbia
4. Alberta, Saskatchewan, Manitoba
5. Northwest Territories, Nunavut, Ontario, Québec, Newfoundland and Labrador
6. Newfoundland and Labrador, Nova Scotia, New Brunswick, Québec, Ontario, Saskatchewan
7. Yukon Territory, British Columbia, Alberta
8. A coniferous tree bears needles and its seeds are in a cone. It does not lose its needles every year; spruce, pine hemlock
9. A deciduous tree bears leaves and then loses them in the autumn of every year; maple, elm, beech
10. It is a large treeless area found above the treeline.

Map of the World #1: Where is Canada? *(page 36)*
1. North America   2. South America
3. Europe   4. Africa
5. Asia   6. Australia
7. Antarctica

1. Arctic Ocean   2. Pacific Ocean
3. Atlantic Ocean   4. Indian Ocean
5. Antarctic Ocean

Map of Canada #2: Canada's Borders *(page 37)*
1. Atlantic Ocean   2. Hudson Bay
3. United States of America
4. Pacific Ocean   5. Alaska
6. Arctic Ocean

Map of Canada #3: Canada's Provinces and Territories *(page 38)*
1. Newfoundland and Labrador
2. Prince Edward Island
3. Nova Scotia   4. New Brunswick
5. Québec   6. Ontario
7. Manitoba   8. Saskatchewan
9. Alberta   10. British Columbia
11. Yukon Territory   12. Northwest Territories
13. Nunavut

CANADIAN PROVINCES AND TERRITORIES

Map of Canada #4: Borders Inside Canada:
(page 39)
Same as Map of Canada #3

Map of Canada #5: Canada's Capital Cities
(page 40)
1. St. John's
2. Charlottetown
3. Halifax
4. Fredericton
5. Toronto
6. Ottawa
7. Québec City
8. Winnipeg
9. Regina
10. Edmonton
11. Victoria
12. Whitehorse
13. Yellowknife
14. Iqaluit

Map of Canada #6: The Physical Regions *(page 41)*
1. Appalachian Highlands
2. St. Lawrence Lowlands
3. Hudson Bay Lowlands
4. Canadian Shield
5. Interior Plains
6. Cordilleran Region
7. Arctic Islands

Map of Canada #9: The Great Lakes *(page 44)*
1. Lake Superior
2. Lake Michigan
3. Lake Huron
4. St. Clair River
5. Lake St. Clair
6. Detroit River
7. Lake Erie
8. Niagara River
9. Lake Ontario
10. St. Lawrence River
11. Ottawa
12. Ontario
13. St. Mary's River
14. United States

Worksheet #16: The Atlantic Provinces
The Atlantic Provinces *(page 57)*
Location:
1: peninsula; island; Cape Breton; Canso; Chignecto;
2: a) Chaleur Bay;   b) Bay of Fundy;
   c) Northumberland Strait; Maine; Québec; Nova Scotia
3: smallest; Gulf of St. Lawrence; Northumberland Strait; bridge; 13.3; Borden; Cape Tormentine
4: Atlantic Ocean; Gulf of St. Lawrence; Cabot Strait; island; mainland

Land Surface:
1. a) The Atlantic Uplands
   b) The Coastal Lowlands
2. a) Cobequid Mountains
   b) Cape Breton Highlands
3. a) Annapolis-Cornwallis Valley
4. Applachian; rugged; Lowland
5. Canadian Shield; Appalachian
6. a) Torngat Mountains
   b) Long Range Mountains
   c) Mealey Mountains

Climate:
1. Labrador
2. Nova Scotia
3. one; hundred
4. colder; warmer

Waterways:
1. isthmus
2. Bay of Fundy; Northumberland Strait
3. Labrador Current
4. Gulf Stream
5. a) Newfoundland and Labrador
   b) New Brunswick
   c) New Brunswick
   d) New Brunswick
   e) New Brunswick
   f) Newfoundland and Labrador
   g) Nova Scotia
   h) Nova Scotia
   i) Prince Edward Island

Agriculture:
1. The soil is not very fertile.
2. Prince Edward Island
3. a) Subsitence farming
   b) fruit farming
   c) potatoes, Prince Edward Island
   d) general farming
   e) apples
   f) fur farming
   g) field crops
   h) dairy farming

Mineral Resources:
1. zinc, silver, lead, potash, coal, gypsum, salt, asbestos, gold, limestone, sand, gravel, tin, peat
2. Cape Breton Island
3. Grand Lake;
4. Newfoundland and Labrador
5. Labrador City, Wabush on Newfoundland and Labrador's mainland

Fishing:
1. a) continental shelf
   b) Grand Banks
   c) cod, Atlantic Salmon
   d) indented, coastline
   e) trawler, dragger, fishing boat
2. lobster, shrimp, flounder, snow crab, scallops, herring
3. aquaculture, fish, farms
4. canning, freezing, salting, smoking
5. United States, Japan, Europe

Cities in the Atlantic Provinces:
1. Charlottetown, East River, harbour, capital
2. Halifax, south, Canso, Sable, harbour, vessels

3. Fredericton; Saint John
4. Saint John, Saint John, Bay, Fundy, harbour
5. St. John's, Avalon, capital
6. Corner Brook, Grand Falls

Map of the Atlantic Provinces: (page 62)
Waterways:
1. Strait of Belle Isle
2. Atlantic Ocean
3. Gulf of St. Lawrence
4. Cabot Strait
5. Strait of Canso
6. Bay of Fundy
7. Saint John River

Provinces:
1. New Brunswick
2. Nova Scotia
3. Prince Edward Island
4.& 5. Newfoundland and Labrador

Cities and Towns:
1. Edmundston
2. Fredericton
3. Saint John
4. Yarmouth
5. Lunenburg
6. Halifax
7. Dartmouth
8. Truro
9. Moncton
10. Borden
11. Charlottetown
12. Souris
13. Sydney
14. Corner Brook
15. Gander
16. Grand Falls
17. St John's

Worksheet #17: The Province of Québec (page 65)
Location: northeastern; Ontario; Labrador; New Brunswick; Maine; New York; Hudson Strait; largest

Surface: St. Lawrence Lowlands; Appalachian Highlands; Canadian Shield; Hudson Bay Lowlands; narrow; band; fertile; Ninety mountain; range ; Laurentian Plateau; James Bay

Climate: varies; long; cold; 120; 160; precipitation; temperatures; hot; humid

Rivers of Québec:
1. Ottawa River
2. St. Maurice River, Ottawa River, Saguenay River, Manicouagon River
3. Harricana River, Nottaway River, George River, Rivière - a - la - Baleine, Koksoak River, Rivière aux Feuilles;
4. Rivière - de - Rupert, Eastmain River, Openaca River, Old Factory River, Fort George River, Roggan River, Grand Rivière - de - la - Baleine, Broadback River
5. Lac St. Jean
6. Lake Minto
7. James Bay
8. Richelieu River, Chaudière River, St. Frances River

Agriculture in Québec:
1. dairy; 40 000; St. Lawrence River; half; butter; cheese
2. oats, barley, wheat, corn
3. apples, blueberries, raspberries, strawberries
4. cabbages, carrots, lettuce, peas, sweet corn, tomatoes, potatoes
5. hogs, poultry, beef cattle
6. maple sugar, maple syrup, sap

Québec's Industries:
1. farming, mining, manufacturing, hydro-electric power, technology, forestry, pulp and paper, fish processing
2. hyrdo-electric power, electricity
3. aerospace industry
4. Noranda
5. Schefferville
6. Noranda, Val-d'Or
7. asbestos, titanium

Québec's Cities:
1. Québec City; walled; oldest; Samuel de Champlain; port; tourist
2. Montréal; island; popular
3. Trois Rivières; halfway
4. Gaspé, Sherbrooke, Rouyn, Rimouski, Sept Iles, Rivière - du - Loup, Val d'Or, Hull

Map of the Province of Québec: (page 68)
Waterways:
1. Hudson Strait
2. Ungava Bay
3. Strait of Belle Isle
4. Strait of Jacques Cartier
5. Strait of Honguedo
6. St. Lawrence River
7. Ottawa River
8. James Bay
9. Hudson Bay

The Provinces:
1. Ontario
2. Québec
3. Newfoundland and Labrador
4. New Brunswick

Cities and Towns:
1. Sept Isles
2. Gaspé
3. Rimouski
4. Rivière du Loup
5. Sherbrooke
6. Hull
7. Montréal
8. Trois Rivières
9. Québec City
10. Rouyn
11. Val d'Or

Worksheet #18: The Province of Ontario (page 71)
Location:
1. Hudson Bay, James Bay, Québec, Great Lakes, United States, Manitoba
2. half

3. Lake Michigan
4. Point Pelee
5. They use the St. Lawrence Seaway to get to the Great Lakes.

Map of Ontario's Boundaries: *(page 72)*
1. Québec
2. Ottawa River
3. St. Lawrence River
4. Lake Ontario
5. Lake Erie
6. Lake St. Clair
7. Lake Huron
8. The United States
9. Lake Superior
10. Ontario
11. James Bay
12. Hudson Bay
13. Manitoba

Surface:
1. four; The Hudson Bay Lowlands, The Canadian Shield, The St. Lawrence Lowlands, The Great Lakes Lowlands
2. Hudson Bay; James Bay; flat; drained; muskegs; permafrost;
3. horseshoe; rocky; lakes; forested; clay; grains; vegetables; beef; dairy cattle; grasslands; minerals; timber; game; animals
4. St. Lawrence River; small; rich; dairy
5. Great Lakes; Erie; Huron; Ontario; fertile; crops; Beef; dairy; Niagara Escarpment; cliff; ridge; Manitoulin Island; Bruce Peninsula; natural; shelter; largest

Climate:
1. winter; spring; summer; autumn
2. Southern; milder; Northern; winds; colder
3. - 5 °C; -25 ° C; 12 °C; 21 ° C; 4. 500 millimetres; twice

Lakes and Rivers of Ontario:
1. Lake Superior
2. Lake St. Clair
3. Lake Ontario
4. Lake of the Woods, Rainy Lake
5. St. Clair River
6. Niagara River
7. Abitibi River
8. Ottawa River
9. St. Mary's River
10. Madawaska River
11. Detroit River
12. Severn River

Agriculture:
1. biggest; livestock; corn
2. Dairy, milk, cheese, yoghurt, cream, ice cream, butter;
3. meat, eggs
4. Niagara, peaches, cherries, plums, pears, grapes, wineries
5. marshes, vegetables, Holland Marsh, Thedford Marsh, Erieau Marsh, Pelee Marsh

Forestry:
1. government, licences, harvest
2. lumber, pulp, paper, twenty, northern, rivers, Huron, Superior, Nipissing; Veneer; Sault Ste. Marie; Thessalon; Plywood; Cochrane; Hearst; New Liskeard; Kirkland Lake; Sturgeon Falls
3. a) Coniferous
   b) Deciduous
4. a) Barges carry the logs to the mills wherever there are no roads.
   b) The logs float in log booms until they are used.

Mining:
1. minerals
2. nickel, cobalt, zinc, copper, gold, cement, platinum, silver, salt
3. a) nickel   b) copper
4. nickel
5. zinc
6. gold

Industries:
1. • located near main cities and waterways in North America
   • close to the United States and its large cities for trading purposes;
   • ocean-going vessels can visit many ports in Ontario
2. The area from Toronto to the Niagara River is called the "Golden Horseshoe"
3. Hamilton, Sault Ste. Marie;
4. automobile, parts
5. Chemical;
6. processing, foods, beverages, Beer, soft drinks, liquor, fruits, vegetables, milk, dairy, mills, wheat, flour, grains, cereals

Ontario's Cities and Towns:
1. Pickering
2. Toronto, Hamilton, Sault Ste. Marie, Thunder Bay;
3. Sudbury
4. Toronto, Peterborough
5. Oshawa, Windsor, Cambridge, Alliston, Oakville;
6. Niagara Falls
7. Toronto, Ottawa, London, Kingston, Peterborough, Kitchener-Waterloo, Hamilton, Guelph
8. Hamilton, Sault Ste. Marie;
9. Toronto
10. Ottawa

Map of Ontario's Cities and Towns: *(page 77)*

1. Thunder Bay
2. Sault Ste. Marie
3. Windsor
4. London
5. Niagara Falls
6. Hamilton
7. Toronto
8. Kingston
9. Ottawa
10. Pembroke
11. North Bay
12. Sudbury
13. Kirkland Lake
14. Timmins
15. Moose Factory

Worksheet #17: The Prairie Provinces *(page 79)*

Location:

a) **Manitoba** - North Border - Nunavut, Hudson Bay;
West Border - Saskatchewan;
East Border - Ontario;
South Border - United States

b) **Saskatchewan** - North Border - Nunavut;
West Border - Alberta;
East Border - Manitoba;
South Border - United States

c) **Alberta** - North Border - Northwest Territories;
West Border - British Columbia;
East Border - Saskatchewan;
South Border - United States

Surface:

1. A slough is a soft, deep, muddy place or mud hole; marshy area
2. Hudson Bay Lowlands; Canadian Shield; Interior Plains; Plateau; Interior Plains; Plateau
3. A prairie is flat land covered with long grass and very few trees
4. Trees are rare on the prairies because it is difficult for them to compete with the grasses and wildflowers. They cannot adapt to the harsh prairie environment
5. The land becomes very dry because there is no rainfall. There is a lack of rain for an extended period of time
6. The soil is rich and fertile.
7. The main causes are drought, flooding and an early frost.

Climate:

1. winter; southeast; north; sunlight; sunniest; short; frost; permafrost; central; snow; rain; overflow; flood; the Red River
2. extreme; long; cold; short; hot; pleasant; wind; continental; rainfall; snowfall; sunshine; drought; northern; colder
3. changeable; snow; July; August; hottest; Indian Summer; warm; cold; October; March; blizzards; windchill; winds; visability; January; quickly; wind direction; west; west; arch of clouds; chinook; warm; dry; 25; disappeared

Lakes and Rivers:

1. Lake Winnipeg
2. Lake Athabaska
3. Lake Manitoba
4. Manitoba
5. Dauphin River, Red River
6. Nelson River , Churchill River, Hayes River
7. South Saskatchewan River

Agriculture:

1. Farming; Wheat; canola; barley; flaxseed; oats; rye; flax; Livestock; 300 hectares; grain; elevators; centre; chemicals; fertilizers; farm machinery
2. third; wheat; oats; canola; sunflowers; lentils; canary seed; cattle; hogs; chickens; turkeys; eggs; milk; honey; vegetables; wheat; 400; fewer; ten; wheat; prices; farming; expenses; government;
3. wheat; canola; cattle; dairy products; vegetables; Japan; United States; changing; larger; fewer; land; machinery; crops;
4. Soil is rich and fertile. They receive a good amount of rainfall. They have a slightly longer growing season. The summer climate is quite warm.

Industries:

1. processed foods; transportation equipment; printing; publishing; clothing; textiles; machinery; Nickel; Copper; Flin Flon; zinc; gold; lead; cobalt; tantalum; tellurium; rivers; lakes; hydro-electric; Winnipeg; Saskatchewan; Nelson; Petroleum; natural gas; The Pas; Pine Falls; Pinawa
2. minerals; petroleum; Potash; fertilizer; uranium; exporter; gold; zinc; salt; clay; oil; gas; Regina; Lloydminister; heavy oil; recover; refine; Lignite; stations; Manufacturing; steel; fertilizer; street sweepers; ambulances; steel-makers; Regina; logging; pulp; paper; small; heavily forested; fishing; whitefish; walleye; pike; United States; Europe
3. "Energy Province"; oil; crude; heavy; sands; sweet; sour; furnaces; exported; sold; food; beverage; chemicals; electronics; machinery; forestry; commercialized; logging roads; overuse; damage; pulp; paper; Athabasca; Peace; herbicides; ecosystem; humans; wildlife; aquatic life; United States; Pacific Rim; Grand Prairie; Hinton; Slave Lake; High Level; White Court; High Prairie; Fox Creek; Athabasca; United States; England; China; Japan; Korea; oil; gas; food; machinery; farm products;

building materials; motor vehicles; retail; mall;
Tourism; scenery; Rocky Mountains; Banff;
Jasper; Waterton

Tourist Attractions:
1. Drumheller, Alberta
2. CFB Moose Jaw, Saskatchewan
3. Churchill, Manitoba;
4. Calgary, Alberta
5. Alberta
6. Banff or Jasper, Alberta
7. Regina, Saskatchewan;
8. Drumheller, Alberta
9. Vegreville, Alberta
10. Jasper, Alberta
11. Churchill, Manitoba
12. Drumheller, Alberta
13. Saskatchewan;
14. Saskatchewan

Map of Manitoba: Cities and Towns: *(page 88)*
1. Lynn Lake
2. Flin Flon
3. The Pas
4. Brandon
5. Portage La Prairie
6. Winnipeg
7. St. Boniface
8. Selkirk
9. Churchill

Lakes:
1. Lake Winnipeg
2. Lake Winnipegosis
3. Lake Manitoba

Rivers:
1. Assiniboine River
2. Souris River
3. Red River
4. Winnipeg River
5. Hayes River
6. Nelson River
7. Churchill River

2. a) capital city of Manitoba, largest city
   b) Manitoba's second largest city
   c) important trading fort during the fur trading period
   d) Copper is mined here
   e) Pulp and paper centre, forestry;
   f) salt water port, place to watch polar bears play in the fall
   g) has one of Canada's longest suspension footbridges

Map of Saskatchewan: Cities and Towns *(page 89)*
1. Uranium City
2. Lloydminister
3. North Battleford
4. Saskatoon
5. Swift Current
6. Moose Jaw
7. Regina
8. Weyburn
9. Estevan
10. Prince Albert
11. Yorkton

Lakes:
1. Lake Athbasca
2. Cree Lake
3. Lac La Ronge
4. Reindeer Lake
5. Wollaston Lake

Rivers:
1. Cree River
2. North Saskatchewan River
3. South Saskatchewan River
4. Qu'Appele River
5. Souris River

2. a) North Saskatchewan River
   b) South Saskatchewan River
   c) North Saskatchewan River
   d) Souris River
   e) Qu'Appelle River
3. a) the largest city in Saskatchewan
   b) the home of W.O. Mitchell, a famous Canadian author who wrote the book *Who Has Seen the Wind?*
   c) one of Saskatchewan's major oil and coal-producing cities
   d) capital of Saskatchewan, second largest in the province, R.C.M.P. school
   e) Prince Albert National Park, contains the cabin and gravesite of Grey Owl (a park ranger)
   f) has the world's largest tomahawk

Map of Alberta: Cities and Towns *(page 90)*
1. Grande Prairie
2. Jasper
3. Banf
4. Calgary
5. Drumheller
6. Medicine Hat
7. Lethbridge
8. Red Deer
9. Wetaskiwun
10. Camrose
11. Lloydminister
12. Edmonton

Lakes:
1. Bistcho Lake
2. Lake Athabasca
3. Lake Claire
4. Utikuma Lake
5. Lesser Slave Lake

Rivers:
1. Peace River
2. Athabasca River
3. North Saskatchewan River
4. Red Deer River
5. Bow River
6. South Saskatchewan River

2. a) North Saskatchewan River
   b) Bow River
   c) South Saskatchewan River
   d) South Saskatchewan River
   e) Red Deer River
   f) Red Deer River
   g) Athabasca River

3. a) holds the Calgary Stampede, largest city in Alberta, has Calgary Olympic Park
   b) a famous national park, beautiful mountain scenery, tourist attraction
   c) Red Deer River Badlands, hoodoos, Museum of Palaeontology
   d) capital city of Alberta;
   e) large oil field
   f) gigantic, aluminum Ukrainian Easter Egg

Worksheet #20: British Columbia *(page 93)*
Location:
1. most westerly province
2. Alberta
3. the Northwest Territories and the Yukon
4. the United States
5. its west coast
6. highly indented
7. part of the state of Alaska

Surface:
1. The Cordilleran Region
2. Pacific Ocean;
3. indented
4. Rocky Mountains
5. Cassair Mountains, Columbia Mountains, Purcell Mountains, Cariboo Mountains, Coast Mountains, Selkirk Mountains, Cascade Mountains, Omineca Mountains
6. Vancouver Island, Queen Charlotte Islands
7. Kicking Horse Pass, Crowsnest Pass, Yellowhead Pass
8. It lies between the Coast Mountains and the Rocky Mountains.

Climate: varied, mountains, lake, different, Vancouver Island, lush, green, forested, Gulf Islands, rainshadow, drier, warmer; interior, hotter, drier, summer, colder, winter; Mild, warm, cool, Moist, autumn, winter, mountains, rain, dry; long, cold, hot

British Columbia's Waterways
2. a) True   b) False   c) False   d) True
   e) True   f) False   g) True   h) True
   i) False   j) False

Map of British Columbia's Waterways: *(page 99)*
1. Pacific Ocean
2. Queen Charlotte Islands
3. Queen Charlotte Strait
4. Juan de Fuca Strait
5. Strait of Georgia
6. Vancouver Island
7. Hecate Strait
8. Laird River
9. Stikine River
10. Nass River
11. Skeena River
12. Babine Lake
13. Williston Lake
14. Fraser River

15. Chilcotin River
16. Quesnel Lake
17. Thompson River
18. Shuswap Lake
19. Okanagan Lake
20. Okanagan River
21. Kootney Lake
22. Columbia River

Forestry: Thousands; exports; harvested; lumber; pulp; paper; shingles; shakes; loggers; truckdrivers; planters; important; conserved; replaced; conflicts; logging; clearcutting; removal; land claims; Forest workers; Resort operators; mill owners; Environmentalists; Commission; forest industry; environment

Mining: mountains; Gold; coal; sulphur; copper; zinc; miners; prospectors; Cassiar; asbestos; Kitimat; sulphur; Coal; southern Okanagan; important; dependable; die; community; main

Energy: energy; resources; five; Pacific Rim; Oil; gas; Westcoast Energy Pipeline; Electricity; Peace; Fraser; Skeena; Columbia; dams; hydro-electric

Fishing: business; thousands; forty; fish; marine; fish-processing; fish; salmon; shellfish; fleets; operators; biologists; workers; farmers; Prince Rupert; Steveston; pinks; sockeye; coho; chum; chinook; highly; fresh; frozen; canned; half; exports; Herring; eggs; roe; spring; roe; female; Japan; delicacy; bodies; animal food; fertilizer; shrinking; commercial; sports; Native

Tourism: scenery; mild; Vancouver; Victoria; mountains; winter; golfers; cyclists; wildlife

British Columbia's Cities:
1. Vancouver; largest; busiest; natural; harbour; freezes; all year; Japan; Asian; Canada's Gateway to the Pacific; beautiful; Pacific Ocean; Coast Mountains; climate; mountains; warm winds; location; climate; Chinese; Indian; Japanese; Pacific Rim
2. capital; city; southern; Vancouver; Island; Canada's City of Flowers; mild; year-round; Butchart; Gardens; famous; old; historic; Empress; Hotel; Totem poles

Map of British Columbia's: Cities and Towns *(page 100)*
1. Prince Rupert
2. Powell River
3. Vancouver
4. Port Alberni
5. Nanaimo
6. Victoria
7. Duncan
8. New Westminister
9. Penticton
10. Kelowna
11. Kamloops
12. Prince George
13. Dawson Creek
14. Kitimat

CANADIAN PROVINCES AND TERRITORIES

<u>Worksheet #21: The Territories</u> *(page 105)*
Location:
The Yukon Territories: northwestern; triangular; Alaska; Northwest Territories ; British Columbia; Beaufort Sea

The Northwest Territories: middle; Yukon; Nunavut; Beaufort sea; British Columbia; Alberta; Saskatchewan

Nunavut Territory: Northwest Territories; Inuit; west; Greenland; Manitoba; Arctic Ocean

Surface:
The Yukon Territory: mountains; plains; plateaus; valleys; Western Cordillera; Interior Plateau; Eastern Cordillera; Arctic Coastal Plain; Saint Elias; Coast; tallest; Mount Logan; highest; Canada; North America; 5 959; Glaciers; ice fields

The Northwest Territories: wilderness; mountains; valleys; forests; ice-capped; three; Arctic Mainland; Mackenzie Valley; Arctic Islands; Canadian Shield; horseshoe; bedrock; minerals

Nunavut: coastline; larger; above the treeline; no trees grow; Canadian Shield

Territorial Climates:
The Yukon Territory: Subartic; - 40 ° C; 30 ° C; long; dark; freeze; middle; December; no; three; five; dry; light; snow; ploughed; pleasant; short; longest; 24 hours; 21 hours; nineteen hours; twilight; sunrise; Land of the Midnight Sun

The Northwest Territories: not; snow; ice; less; southern; blown; winds; rains; desert; warm; hot; 21 ° C; 40 ° C; cold; winds; long; Arctic; nine; celebrate; brighter; warmer; longer; short; quickly; long; hours

Nunavut: coldest; nine; -30 ° C; chilling winds; blizzards; blowing winds; colder; warm; 30 ° C; summer; toward; closest; continual; sunlight; midnight; opposite; away; northermost; constant darkness

Industries:
The Yukon Territory: backbone; gold; Klondike; Gold; ten ; Lead; zinc; ore; mined out; world; too low

Tourism: second; history; wilderness; adventure; tours canoeing; rafting; employs; quarter

The Government: government; highest; federal; territorial; municipal

The Fur Trade: trapping; trading; Hudson Bay Company; some; uncertain; fluctuate; demand; decreased; Beavers; martens; lynxes; foxes; minks
Forestry: slowly; fifty; Forest fires; lightning; not; three; seasonal; Watson Lake; Whitehorse

Farming: poor; rainfall; permafrost; long; sunlight; quickly; important; successful; vegetables; field crops; Whitehorse; commercial; vegetables; seeds; pigs; chickens; goats; cattle; reindeer; Pelly; crops; cattle

Fishing: important; chinook; chum; sold; Trout; Arctic char; Sport; dollars; Anglers; waters;

The Northwest Territories' Industries:
Mining: mineral; important; development; expensive; extract; transport; government; most; important; more money;

Oil and Gas: offshore; oil; onshore; gas; active; Bent Horn; Pointed Mountain; Norman Wells; artificial islands; pipeline

Trapping and Hunting: oldest; most important; changes in fashions; against trapping and killing animals; beaver; arctic; red; lynx; marten; mink; muskrat; wolf; wolverine; caribou; moose; musk-ox; seal; whale; grouse; ptarmigan; duck; goose; harvested; exported; Sportshunting; hunters; big game; polar bear hunt; $17 000; Inuit; good;

Fishing: lakes; streams; commercial; tourists; sport; release; stocks; lodges; Great Bear Lake; Great Slave Lake; commercial

Forestry: not; limited; treeline; useful; sawmills; shortage; lack; knowledgeable

Farming: farms; Hay River; chicken; egg; cattle; bison; market garden; Fort Simpson; Fort Smith; Tuktoyaktuk; reindeer; meat; antlers; Hydroponic; greenhouses; community

Nunavut's Industries:
remote; transportation; slow; expensive; industries; economy

The Inuit Lifestyle:
variety; construction workers; tour guides; artisans; tapestries; carvings; sculptures

Government Jobs: government; doctors; nurses

Tourism: fastest; work; outfitters; rents; tents; kayaks; explore; unspoiled; guides; paddle; kayak; hiking; climb

Construction: expanding; rapidly; busy; schools; offices; community; homes

Mining: rich deposits; lead; zinc; Little Cornwallis Island; Arctic Bay; Lupin Mine; Contwoyto Lake; gold; Oil; gas; Bent Horn; Cameron Island

Manufacturing: factories; processing; meat; fish; build; create

The Yukon's Cities and Towns:
1. Whitehorse; west; Yukon; modern; log cabins; log-scrapers; S.S. Klondike; sternwheelers;
2. Dawson City; Yukon; Klondike; wide; boardwalks; Robert Service's; houses; stores; hotels

The Northwest Territories' Cities and Towns
1. Yellowknife; Great Slave Lake; gateway; streets; skyscrapers; modern; prospectors'; quonset; makeshift; prospectors; Ingraham Trail; Great Slave Lake; Mackenzie River
2. Fort Smith; second; national; Wood Buffalo National Park; Rafters; rapids; portage; route
3. Inuvik; largest; north; modern; Aklavik; Delta

The Cities and Towns of Nunavut:
1. small; few; far; 22 000; isolated; Iqaluit; largest; capital; city; Baffin; Toonik Tyme; Pond Inlet; history; modern; permanently; buildings; completely; pipes; water; fuel; above

Map of the Yukon: Cities and Towns (page 113)
1. Old Crow
2. Dawson City
3. Carmacks
4. Haines Junction
5. Faro
6. Whitehorse
7. Carcross
8. Teslin
9. Watson lake

Map of The Northwest Territories: Cities and Towns (page 114)
1. Tuktayaktuk
2. Inuvik
3. Norman Wells
4. Deline
5. Fort Norman
6. Wrigley
7. Fort Simpson
8. Rae
9. Yellowknife
10. Fort Resolution
11. Pine Point
12. Fort Smith
13. Hay River
14. Fort Laird

Map of the Communities in Nunavut: (page 115)
1. Resolute
2. Pond Inlet
3. Pangnirtung
4. Iqaluit
5. Cape Dorset
6. Arviat
7. Whale Cove
8. Rankin Inlet
9. Chesterfield Inlet
10. Baker Lake
11. Repulse Bay
12. Gjoa Haven
13. Coppermine
14. Cambridge Bay
15. Alert

Publication Listing

Code #	Title and Grade
SSC1-12	A Time of Plenty Gr. 2
SSN1-92	Abel's Island NS Gr. 4-6
SSF1-16	Aboriginal Peoples of Canada Gr. 7-8
SSK1-31	Addition & Subtraction Drills Gr. 1-3
SSK1-28	Addition Drills Gr. 1-3
SSY1-04	Addition Gr. 1-3
SSN1-174	Adv. of Huckle Berry Finn NS Gr. 7-8
SSB1-63	African Animals Gr 4-6
SSB1-29	All About Bears Gr. 1-2
SSF1-08	All About Boats Gr. 2-3
SSJ1-02	All About Canada Gr. 2
SSB1-54	All About Cattle Gr. 4-6
SSN1-10	All About Colours Gr. P-1
SSB1-93	All About Dinosaurs Gr. 2
SSN1-14	All About Dragons Gr. 3-5
SSB1-07	All About Elephants Gr. 3-4
SSB1-68	All About Fish Gr. 4-6
SSN1-39	All About Giants Gr. 2-3
SSH1-15	All About Jobs Gr. 1-3
SSH1-05	All About Me Gr. 1
SSA1-02	All About Mexico Gr. 4-6
SSR1-28	All About Nouns Gr. 5-7
SSF1-09	All About Planes Gr. 2-3
SSB1-33	All About Plants Gr. 2-3
SSR1-29	All About Pronouns Gr. 5-7
SSB1-12	All About Rabbits Gr. 2-3
SSB1-58	All About Spiders Gr. 4-6
SSA1-03	All About the Desert Gr. 4-6
SSA1-04	All About the Ocean Gr. 5-7
SSZ1-01	All About the Olympics Gr. 2-4
SSB1-49	All About the Sea Gr. 4-6
SSK1-06	All About Time Gr. 4-6
SSF1-07	All About Trains Gr. 2-3
SSH1-18	All About Transportation Gr. 2
SSB1-01	All About Trees Gr. 4-6
SSB1-61	All About Weather Gr. 7-8
SSB1-06	All About Whales Gr. 3-4
SSPC-26	All Kinds of Clocks B/W Pictures
SSB1-110	All Kinds of Structures Gr. 1
SSH1-19	All Kinds of Vehicles Gr. 3
SSF1-01	Amazing Aztecs Gr. 4-6
SSB1-92	Amazing Earthworms Gr. 2-3
SSJ1-50	Amazing Facts in Cdn History Gr. 4-6
SSB1-32	Amazing Insects Gr. 4-6
SSN1-132	Amelia Bedelia–Camping NS 1-3
SSN1-68	Amelia Bedelia NS 1-3
SSN1-155	Amelia Bedelia-Surprise Shower NS 1-3
SSA1-13	America The Beautiful Gr. 4-6
SSN1-57	Amish Adventure NS 7-8
SSF1-02	Ancient China Gr. 4-6
SSF1-18	Ancient Egypt Gr. 4-6
SSF1-21	Ancient Greece Gr. 4-6
SSF1-19	Ancient Rome Gr. 4-6
SSQ1-06	Animal Town – Big Book Pkg 1-3
SSQ1-02	Animals Prepare Winter – Big Book Pkg 1-3
SSN1-150	Animorphs the Invasion NS 4-6
SSN1-53	Anne of Green Gables NS 7-8
SSB1-40	Apple Celebration Gr. 4-6
SSB1-04	Apple Mania Gr. 2-3
SSB1-38	Apples are the Greatest Gr. P-K
SSB1-59	Arctic Animals Gr. 4-6
SSN1-162	Arnold Lobel Author Study Gr. 2-3
SSPC-22	Australia B/W Pictures
SSA1-05	Australia Gr. 5-8
SSM1-03	Autumn in the Woodlot Gr. 2-3
SSM1-08	Autumn Wonders Gr. 1
SSN1-41	Baby Sister for Frances NS 1-3
SSPC-19	Back to School B/W Pictures
SSC1-33	Back to School Gr. 2-3
SSN1-224	Banner in the Sky NS 7-8
SSN1-36	Bargain for Frances NS 1-3
SSB1-82	Bats Gr. 4-6
SSN1-71	BB – Drug Free Zone NS Gr. 1-3
SSN1-88	BB – In the Freaky House NS 1-3
SSN1-78	BB – Media Madness NS 1-3
SSN1-69	BB – Wheelchair Commando NS 1-3
SSN1-119	Be a Perfect Person-3 Days NS 4-6
SSC1-15	Be My Valentine Gr. 1
SSD1-01	Be Safe Not Sorry Gr. P-1
SSN1-09	Bear Tales Gr. 2-4
SSB1-28	Bears Gr. 4-6
SSN1-202	Bears in Literature Gr. 1-3
SSN1-40	Beatrix Potter Gr. 2-4
SSN1-129	Beatrix Potter: Activity Biography Gr. 2-4
SSB1-47	Beautiful Bugs Gr. 1
SSB1-21	Beavers Gr. 3-5
SSN1-257	Because of Winn-Dixie NS Gr. 4-6
SSR1-53	Beginning Manuscript Gr. Pk-2
SSR1-54	Beginning Cursive Gr. 2-4
SSR1-57	Beginning and Practice Manuscript Gr. PK-2
SSR1-58	Beginning and Practice Cursive Gr. 2-4
SSN1-33	Bedtime for Frances NS 1-3
SSN1-114	Best Christmas Pageant Ever NS Gr. 4-6
SSN1-32	Best Friends for Frances NS Gr. 1-3
SSB1-39	Best Friends Pets Gr. P-K
SSN1-185	BFG NS Gr. 4-6
SSJ1-61	Big Book of Canadian Celebrations Gr. 1-3
SSJ1-62	Big Book of Canadian Celebrations Gr. 4-6
SSN1-35	Birthday for Frances NS Gr. 1-3
SSN1-107	Borrowers NS Gr. 4-6
SSC1-16	Bouquet of Valentines Gr. 2
SSN1-29	Bread & Jam for Frances NS Gr. 1-3
SSN1-63	Bridge to Terabithia NS Gr. 4-6
SSY1-24	BTS Numeración Gr. 1-3
SSY1-25	BTS Adición Gr. 1-3
SSY1-26	BTS Sustracción Gr. 1-3
SSY1-27	BTS Fonética Gr. 1-3
SSY1-28	BTS Leer para Entender Gr. 1-3
SSY1-29	BTS Uso de las Mayúsculas y Reglas de Puntuación Gr. 1-3
SSY1-30	BTS Composición de Oraciones Gr. 1-3
SSY1-31	BTS Composici13n de Historias Gr. 1-3
SSN1-256	Bud, Not Buddy NS Gr. 4-6
SSB1-31	Bugs, Bugs & More Bugs Gr. 2-3
SSR1-07	Building Word Families L.V. Gr. 1-2
SSR1-05	Building Word Families S.V. Gr. 1-2
SSN1-204	Bunnicula NS Gr. 4-6
SSB1-80	Butterflies & Caterpillars Gr. 1-2
SSN1-164	Call It Courage NS Gr. 7-8
SSN1-67	Call of the Wild NS Gr. 7-8
SSJ1-41	Canada & It's Trading Partners 6-8
SSPC-28	Canada B/W Pictures
SSN1-173	Canada Geese Quilt NS Gr. 4-6
SSJ1-01	Canada Gr. 1
SSJ1-33	Canada's Capital Cities Gr. 4-6
SSJ1-43	Canada's Confederation Gr. 7-8
SSF1-04	Canada's First Nations Gr. 7-8
SSJ1-51	Canada's Landmarks Gr. 1-3
SSJ1-48	Canada's Landmarks Gr. 4-6
SSJ1-60	Canada's Links to the World Gr. 5-8
SSJ1-42	Canada's Traditions & Celeb. Gr. 1-3
SSB1-45	Canadian Animals Gr. 1-2
SSJ1-37	Canadian Arctic Inuit Gr. 2-3
SSJ1-53	Canadian Black History Gr. 4-8
SSJ1-57	Canadian Comprehension Gr. 1-2
SSJ1-58	Canadian Comprehension Gr. 3-4
SSJ1-59	Canadian Comprehension Gr. 5-6
SSJ1-46	Canadian Industries Gr. 4-6
SSK1-12	Canadian Problem Solving Gr. 4-6
SSJ1-38	Canadian Provinces & Terr. Gr. 4-6
SSY1-07	Capitalization & Punctuation Gr. 1-3
SSN1-198	Captain Courageous NS Gr. 7-8
SSK1-11	Cars Problem Solving Gr. 3-4
SSN1-154	Castle in the Attic NS Gr. 4-6
SSF1-31	Castles & Kings Gr. 4-6
SSN1-144	Cat Ate My Gymsuit NS Gr. 4-6
SSPC-38	Cats B/W Pictures
SSB1-50	Cats – Domestic & Wild Gr. 4-6
SSN1-34	Cats in Literature Gr. 3-6
SSN1-212	Cay NS Gr. 7-8
SSM1-09	Celebrate Autumn Gr. 4-6
SSC1-39	Celebrate Christmas Gr. 4-6
SSC1-31	Celebrate Easter Gr. 4-6
SSC1-23	Celebrate Shamrock Day Gr. 2
SSM1-11	Celebrate Spring Gr. 4-6
SSC1-13	Celebrate Thanksgiving R. 3-4
SSM1-06	Celebrate Winter Gr. 4-6
SSB1-107	Cells, Tissues & Organs Gr. 7-8
SSB1-101	Characteristics of Flight Gr. 4-6
SSN1-66	Charlie & Chocolate Factory NS Gr. 4-6
SSN1-23	Charlotte's Web NS Gr. 4-6
SSB1-37	Chicks N'Ducks Gr. 2-4
SSA1-09	China Today Gr. 5-8
SSN1-70	Chocolate Fever NS Gr. 4-6
SSN1-241	Chocolate Touch NS Gr. 4-6
SSC1-38	Christmas Around the World Gr. 4-6
SSPC-42	Christmas B/W Pictures
SST1-08A	Christmas Gr. JK/SK
SST1-08B	Christmas Gr. 1
SST1-08C	Christmas Gr. 2-3
SSC1-04	Christmas Magic Gr. 1
SSC1-03	Christmas Tales Gr. 2-3
SSG1-06	Cinematography Gr. 5-8
SSPC-13	Circus B/W Pictures
SSF1-03	Circus Magic Gr. 3-4
SSJ1-52	Citizenship/Immigration Gr. 4-8
SSN1-104	Classical Poetry Gr. 7-12
SSN1-227	Color Gr. 1-3
SSN1-203	Colour Gr. 1-3
SSN1-135	Come Back Amelia Bedelia NS 1-3
SSH1-11	Community Helpers Gr. 1-3
SSK1-02	Concept Cards & Activities Gr. P-1
SSN1-183	Copper Sunrise NS Gr. 7-8
SSN1-86	Corduroy & Pocket Corduroy NS 1-3
SSN1-124	Could Dracula Live in Wood NS 4-6
SSN1-148	Cowboy's Don't Cry NS Gr. 7-8
SSR1-01	Creativity with Food Gr. 4-8
SSB1-34	Creatures of the Sea Gr. 2-4
SSN1-208	Curse of the Viking Grave NS 7-8
SSN1-134	Danny Champion of World NS 4-6
SSN1-98	Danny's Run NS Gr. 7-8
SSK1-21	Data Management Gr. 4-6
SSB1-53	Dealing with Dinosaurs Gr. 4-6
SSN1-178	Dear Mr. Henshaw NS Gr. 4-6
SSB1-22	Deer Gr. 3-5
SSPC-20	Desert B/W Pictures
SSJ1-40	Development of Western Canada 7-8
SSA1-16	Development of Manufacturing 7-9
SSN1-105	Dicken's Christmas NS Gr. 7-8
SSN1-62	Different Dragons NS Gr. 4-6
SSPC-21	Dinosaurs B/W Pictures
SSB1-16	Dinosaurs Gr. 1
SST1-02A	Dinosaurs Gr. JK/SK
SST1-02B	Dinosaurs Gr. 1
SST1-02 C	Dinosaurs Gr. 2-3
SSN1-175	Dinosaurs in Literature Gr. 1-3
SSJ1-26	Discover Nova Scotia Gr. 5-7
SSJ1-36	Discover Nunavut Territory Gr. 5-7
SSJ1-25	Discover Ontario Gr. 5-7
SSJ1-24	Discover PEI Gr. 5-7
SSJ1-22	Discover Québec Gr. 5-7
SSL1-01	Discovering the Library Gr. 2-3
SSB1-106	Diversity of Living Things Gr. 4-6
SSK1-27	Division Drills Gr. 4-6
SSB1-30	Dogs – Wild & Tame Gr. 4-6
SSPC-31	Dogs B/W Pictures
SSN1-196	Dog's Don't Tell Jokes NS Gr. 4-6
SSN1-182	Door in the Wall NS Gr. 4-6
SSB1-87	Down by the Sea Gr. 1-3
SSN1-189	Dr. Jeckyll & Mr. Hyde NS Gr. 4-6
SSG1-07	Dragon Trivia Gr. P-8
SSN1-102	Dragon's Egg NS Gr. 4-6
SSN1-16	Dragons in Literature Gr. 3-6
SSC1-06	Early Christmas Gr. 3-5
SSB1-109	Earth's Crust Gr. 6-8
SSC1-21	Easter Adventures Gr. 3-4
SSC1-17	Easter Delights Gr. P-K
SSC1-19	Easter Surprises Gr. 1
SSPC-12	Egypt B/W Pictures
SSN1-255	Egypt Game NS Gr. 4-6
SSF1-28	Egyptians Today & Yesterday Gr. 2-3
SSJ1-49	Elections in Canada Gr. 4-8
SSB1-108	Electricity Gr. 4-6
SSN1-02	Elves & the Shoemaker NS Gr. 1-3
SSH1-14	Emotions Gr. P-2
SSB1-85	Energy Gr. 4-6
SSN1-108	English Language Gr. 10-12
SSN1-156	Enjoying Eric Wilson Series Gr. 5-7
SSB1-64	Environment Gr. 4-6
SSR1-12	ESL Teaching Ideas Gr. K-8
SSN1-258	Esperanza Rising NS Gr. 4-6
SSR1-22	Exercises in Grammar Gr. 6
SSR1-23	Exercises in Grammar Gr. 7
SSR1-24	Exercises in Grammar Gr. 8
SSF1-20	Exploration Gr. 4-6
SSF1-15	Explorers & Mapmakers of Can. 7-8
SSJ1-54	Exploring Canada Gr. 1-3
SSJ1-56	Exploring Canada Gr. 1-6
SSJ1-55	Exploring Canada Gr. 4-6
SSH1-20	Exploring My School & Community 1
SSPC-39	Fables B/W Pictures
SSN1-15	Fables Gr. 4-6
SSN1-04	Fairy Tale Magic Gr. 3-5
SSPC-11	Fairy Tales B/W Pictures
SSN1-11	Fairy Tales Gr. 1-2
SSN1-199	Family Under the Bridge NS Gr. 4-6
SSPC-41	Famous Canadians B/W Pictures
SSJ1-12	Famous Canadians Gr. 4-8
SSN1-210	Fantastic Mr. Fox NS Gr. 4-6
SSB1-36	Fantastic Plants Gr. 4-6
SSPC-04	Farm Animals B/W Pictures
SSB1-15	Farm Animals Gr. 1-2
SST1-03A	Farm Gr. JK/SK
SST1-03B	Farm Gr. 1
SST1-03C	Farm Gr. 2-3
SSJ1-05	Farming Community Gr. 3-4
SSB1-44	Farmyard Friends Gr. P-K
SSJ1-45	Fathers of Confederation Gr. 4-8
SSB1-19	Feathered Friends Gr. 4-6
SST1-05A	February Gr. JK/SK
SST1-05B	February Gr. 1
SST1-05C	February Gr. 2-3
SSN1-03	Festival of Fairytales Gr. 3-5
SSC1-36	Festivals Around the World Gr. 2-3
SSN1-168	First 100 Sight Words Gr. 1
SSC1-32	First Days at School Gr. 1
SSJ1-06	Fishing Community Gr. 3-4
SSN1-170	Flowers for Algernon NS Gr. 7-8
SSN1-261	Flat Stanley NS Gr. 1-3
SSN1-128	Fly Away Home NS Gr. 4-6
SSD1-05	Food: Fact, Fun & Fiction Gr. 1-3
SSD1-06	Food: Nutrition & Invention Gr. 4-6
SSB1-118	Force and Motion Gr. 1-3
SSB1-119	Force and Motion Gr. 4-6
SSB1-25	Foxes Gr. 3-5
SSN1-263	Fractured Fairy Tales NS Gr. 1-3
SSN1-172	Freckle Juice NS Gr. 1-3
SSB1-43	Friendly Frogs Gr. 1
SSN1-260	Frindle NS Gr. 4-6
SSB1-89	Fruits & Seeds Gr. 4-6
SSN1-137	Fudge-a-Mania NS Gr. 4-6
SSB1-14	Fun on the Farm Gr. 3-4
SSR1-49	Fun with Phonics Gr. 1-3
SSPC-06	Garden Flowers B/W Pictures
SSK1-03	Geometric Shapes Gr. 2-5
SSC1-18	Get the Rabbit Habit Gr. 1-2
SSN1-209	Giver, The NS Gr. 7-8
SSN1-190	Go Jump in the Pool NS Gr. 4-6
SSG1-03	Goal Setting Gr. 6-8
SSG1-08	Gr. 3 Test – Parent Guide
SSG1-99	Gr. 3 Test – Teacher Guide
SSG1-09	Gr. 6 Language Test–Parent Guide
SSG1-97	Gr. 6 Language Test–Teacher Guide
SSG1-10	Gr. 6 Math Test – Parent Guide
SSG1-96	Gr. 6 Math Test – Teacher Guide
SSG1-98	Gr. 6 Math/Lang. Test–Teacher Guide
SSK1-14	Graph for all Seasons Gr. 1-3
SSN1-117	Great Brain NS Gr. 4-6
SSN1-90	Great Expectations NS Gr. 7-8
SSN1-169	Great Gilly Hopkins NS Gr. 4-6
SSN1-197	Great Science Fair Disaster NS Gr. 4-6
SSN1-138	Greek Mythology Gr. 7-8
SSN1-113	Green Gables Detectives NS 4-6
SSC1-26	Groundhog Celebration Gr. 2
SSC1-25	Groundhog Day Gr. 1
SSB1-113	Growth & Change in Animals Gr. 2-3
SSB1-114	Growth & Change in Plants Gr. 2-3
SSB1-48	Guinea Pigs & Friends Gr. 3-5
SSB1-104	Habitats Gr. 4-6
SSPC-18	Halloween B/W Pictures
SST1-04A	Halloween Gr. JK/SK
SST1-04B	Halloween Gr. 1
SST1-04C	Halloween Gr. 2-3
SSC1-10	Halloween Gr. 4-6
SSC1-08	Halloween Happiness Gr. 1
SSC1-29	Halloween Spirits Gr. P-K
SSY1-13	Handwriting Manuscript Gr 1-3
SSY1-14	Handwriting Cursive Gr. 1-3
SSC1-42	Happy Valentines Day Gr. 3
SSN1-205	Harper Moon NS Gr. 7-8
SSN1-123	Harriet the Spy NS Gr. 4-6
SSC1-11	Harvest Time Wonders Gr. 1
SSN1-136	Hatchet NS Gr. 7-8
SSC1-09	Haunting Halloween Gr. 2-3
SSN1-91	Hawk & Stretch NS Gr. 4-6
SSC1-30	Hearts & Flowers Gr. P-K
SSN1-22	Heidi NS Gr. 4-6
SSN1-120	Help I'm Trapped in My NS Gr. 4-6
SSN1-24	Henry & the Clubhouse NS Gr. 4-6
SSN1-184	Hobbit NS Gr. 7-8
SSN1-122	Hoboken Chicken Emerg. NS 4-6
SSN1-250	Holes NS Gr. 4-6
SSN1-116	How Can a Frozen Detective NS 4-6
SSN1-89	How Can I be a Detective if I NS 4-6
SSN1-96	How Come the Best Clues... NS 4-6

Publication Listing

Code #	Title and Grade
SSN1-133	How To Eat Fried Worms NS Gr.4-6
SSR1-48	How To Give a Presentation Gr. 4-6
SSN1-125	How To Teach Writing Through 7-9
SSR1-10	How To Write a Composition 6-10
SSR1-09	How To Write a Paragraph 5-10
SSR1-08	How To Write an Essay Gr. 7-12
SSR1-03	How To Write Poetry & Stories 4-6
SSD1-01	Human Body Gr. 2-4
SSD1-02	Human Body Gr. 4-6
SSN1-25	I Want to Go Home NS Gr. 4-6
SSH1-06	I'm Important Gr. 2-3
SSH1-07	I'm Unique Gr. 4-6
SSF1-05	In Days of Yore Gr. 4-6
SSF1-06	In Pioneer Days Gr. 2-4
SSM1-10	In the Wintertime Gr. 2
SSB1-41	Incredible Dinosaurs Gr. P-1
SSN1-177	Incredible Journey NS Gr. 4-6
SSN1-100	Indian in the Cupboard NS Gr. 4-6
SSPC-05	Insects B/W Pictures
SSPC-10	Inuit B/W Pictures
SSJ1-10	Inuit Community Gr. 3-4
SSN1-85	Ira Sleeps Over NS Gr. 1-3
SSN1-93	Iron Man NS Gr. 4-6
SSN1-193	Island of the Blue Dolphins NS 4-6
SSB1-11	It's a Dogs World Gr. 2-3
SSM1-05	It's a Marshmallow World Gr. 3
SSK1-05	It's About Time Gr. 2-4
SSC1-41	It's Christmas Time Gr. 3
SSH1-04	It's Circus Time Gr. 1
SSC1-43	It's Groundhog Day Gr. 3
SSB1-75	It's Maple Syrup Time Gr. 2-4
SSC1-40	It's Trick or Treat Time Gr. 2
SSN1-65	James & The Giant Peach NS 4-6
SSN1-106	Jane Eyre NS Gr. 7-8
SSPC-25	Japan B/W Pictures
SSA1-06	Japan Gr. 5-8
SSN1-264	Journey to the Centre of the Earth NS Gr. 7-8
SSC1-05	Joy of Christmas Gr. 2
SSN1-161	Julie of the Wolves NS Gr. 7-8
SSB1-81	Jungles Gr. 2-3
SSE1-02	Junior Music for Fall Gr. 4-6
SSE1-05	Junior Music for Spring Gr. 4-6
SSE1-06	Junior Music for Winter Gr. 4-6
SSR1-62	Just for Boys - Reading Comprehension Gr. 3-6
SSR1-63	Just for Boys - Reading Comprehension Gr. 6-8
SSN1-151	Kate NS Gr. 4-6
SSN1-95	Kidnapped in the Yukon NS Gr. 4-6
SSN1-141	Kids at Bailey School Gr. 2-4
SSN1-176	King of the Wind NS Gr. 4-6
SSF1-29	Klondike Gold Rush Gr. 4-6
SSF1-33	Labour Movement in Canada Gr. 7-8
SSN1-152	Lamplighter NS Gr. 4-6
SSB1-98	Learning About Dinosaurs Gr. 3
SSN1-38	Learning About Giants Gr. 4-6
SSK1-22	Learning About Measurement Gr. 1-3
SSB1-46	Learning About Mice Gr. 3-5
SSK1-09	Learning About Money CDN Gr. 1-3
SSK1-19	Learning About Money USA Gr. 1-3
SSK1-23	Learning About Numbers Gr. 1-3
SSB1-69	Learning About Rocks & Soils Gr. 2-3
SSK1-08	Learning About Shapes Gr. 1-3
SSB1-100	Learning About Simple Machines 1-3
SSK1-04	Learning About the Calendar Gr. 2-3
SSK1-10	Learning About Time Gr. 1-3
SSH1-17	Learning About Transportation Gr. 1
SSB1-02	Leaves Gr. 2-3
SSN1-50	Legends Gr. 4-6
SSC1-27	Lest We Forget Gr. 4-6
SSJ1-13	Let's Look at Canada Gr. 4-6
SSJ1-16	Let's Visit Alberta Gr. 2-4
SSJ1-15	Let's Visit British Columbia Gr. 2-4
SSJ1-03	Let's Visit Canada Gr. 3
SSJ1-18	Let's Visit Manitoba Gr. 2-4
SSJ1-21	Let's Visit New Brunswick Gr. 2-4
SSJ1-27	Let's Visit NFLD & Labrador Gr. 2-4
SSJ1-30	Let's Visit North West Terr. Gr. 2-4
SSJ1-20	Let's Visit Nova Scotia Gr. 2-4
SSJ1-34	Let's Visit Nunavut Gr. 2-4
SSJ1-17	Let's Visit Ontario Gr. 2-4
SSQ1-08	Let's Visit Ottawa Big Book Pkg 1-3
SSJ1-19	Let's Visit PEI Gr. 2-4
SSJ1-31	Let's Visit Québec Gr. 2-4
SSJ1-14	Let's Visit Saskatchewan Gr. 2-4
SSJ1-28	Let's Visit Yukon Gr. 2-4
SSN1-130	Life & Adv. of Santa Claus NS 7-8
SSB1-10	Life in a Pond Gr. 3-4
SSF1-30	Life in the Middle Ages Gr. 7-8
SSB1-103	Light & Sound Gr. 4-6
SSN1-219	Light in the Forest NS Gr. 7-8
SSN1-121	Light on Hogback Hill NS Gr. 4-6
SSN1-46	Lion, Witch & the Wardrobe NS 4-6
SSR1-51	Literature Response Forms Gr. 1-3
SSR1-52	Literature Response Forms Gr. 4-6
SSN1-28	Little House Big Woods NS 4-6
SSN1-233	Little House on the Prairie NS 4-6
SSN1-111	Little Women NS Gr. 7-8
SSN1-115	Live from the Fifth Grade NS 4-6
SSN1-141	Look Through My Window NS 4-6
SSN1-112	Look! Visual Discrimination Gr. P-1
SSN1-61	Lost & Found Gr. 4-6
SSN1-109	Lost in the Barrens NS Gr. 7-8
SSJ1-08	Lumbering Community Gr. 3-4
SSN1-167	Magic School Bus Gr. 1-3
SSN1-247	Magic Treehouse Gr. 1-3
SSB1-78	Magnets Gr. 3-5
SSD1-03	Making Sense of Our Senses K-1
SSN1-146	Mama's Going to Buy You a NS 4-6
SSB1-94	Mammals Gr. 1
SSB1-95	Mammals Gr. 2
SSB1-96	Mammals Gr. 3
SSB1-97	Mammals Gr. 5-6
SSN1-160	Maniac Magee NS Gr. 4-6
SSA1-19	Mapping Activities & Outlines! 4-8
SSA1-17	Mapping Skills Gr. 1-3
SSA1-07	Mapping Skills Gr. 4-6
SST1-10A	March Gr. JK/SK
SST1-10B	March Gr. 1
SST1-10C	March Gr. 2-3
SSB1-57	Marvellous Marsupials Gr. 4-6
SSK1-01	Math Signs & Symbols Gr. 1-3
SSB1-116	Matter & Materials Gr. 1-3
SSB1-117	Matter & Materials Gr. 4-6
SSH1-03	Me, I'm Special! Gr. P-1
SSK1-16	Measurement Gr. 4-8
SSC1-02	Medieval Christmas Gr. 4-6
SSPC-09	Medieval Life B/W Pictures
SSC1-07	Merry Christmas Gr. P-K
SSK1-15	Metric Measurement Gr. 4-6
SSN1-13	Mice in Literature Gr. 3-5
SSB1-70	Microscopy Gr. 4-6
SSN1-180	Midnight Fox NS Gr. 4-6
SSN1-243	Midwife's Apprentice NS Gr. 4-6
SSJ1-07	Mining Community Gr. 3-4
SSK1-17	Money Talks – Cdn Gr. 1-3
SSK1-18	Money Talks – USA Gr. 1-3
SSB1-56	Monkeys & Apes Gr. 4-6
SSN1-43	Monkeys in Literature Gr. 2-4
SSN1-54	Monster Mania Gr. 4-6
SSN1-97	Mouse & the Motorcycle Gr. 4-6
SSN1-94	Mr. Poppers Penguins NS Gr. 4-6
SSN1-201	Mrs. Frisby & Rats NS Gr. 4-6
SSR1-13	Milti-Level Spelling Program Gr. 3-6
SSR1-26	Multi-Level Spelling USA Gr. 3-6
SSK1-31	Addition & Subtraction Drills 1-3
SSK1-32	Multiplication & Division Drills 4-6
SSK1-30	Multiplication Drills Gr. 4-6
SSA1-14	My Country! The USA! Gr. 2-4
SSN1-186	My Side of the Mountain NS 7-8
SSN1-58	Mysteries, Monsters & Magic Gr. 6-8
SSN1-37	Mystery at Blackrock Island NS 7-8
SSN1-80	Mystery House NS 4-6
SSN1-103	Nate the Great & Sticky Case NS 1-3
SSF1-23	Native People of North America 4-6
SSF1-25	New France Part 1 Gr. 7-8
SSF1-27	New France Part 2 Gr. 7-8
SSA1-10	New Zealand Gr. 4-8
SSN1-51	Newspapers Gr. 5-8
SSN1-47	No Word for Goodbye NS Gr. 7-8
SSPC-03	North American Animals B/W Pictures
SSF1-22	North American Natives Gr. 2-4
SSN1-75	Novel Ideas Gr. 4-6
SST1-06A	November JK/SK
SST1-06B	November Gr. 1
SST1-06C	November Gr. 2-3
SSN1-244	Number the Stars NS Gr. 4-6
SSY1-03	Numeration Gr. 1-3
SSPC-14	Nursery Rhymes B/W Pictures
SSN1-12	Nursery Rhymes Gr. P-1
SSN1-59	On the Banks of Plum Creek NS 4-6
SSN1-220	One in Middle Green Kangaroo NS 1-3
SSN1-145	One to Grow On NS Gr. 4-6
SSB1-27	Opossums Gr. 3-5
SSJ1-23	Ottawa Gr. 7-9
SSJ1-39	Our Canadian Governments Gr. 5-8
SSF1-14	Our Global Heritage Gr. 4-6
SSH1-12	Our Neighbourhoods Gr. 4-6
SSB1-72	Our Trash Gr. 2-3
SSB1-51	Our Universe Gr. 5-8
SSB1-86	Outer Space Gr. 1-2
SSA1-18	Outline Maps of the World Gr. 1-8
SSB1-67	Owls Gr. 4-6
SSN1-31	Owls in the Family NS Gr. 4-6
SSL1-02	Oxbridge Owl & The Library Gr. 4-6
SSB1-71	Pandas, Polar & Penguins Gr. 4-6
SSN1-52	Paperbag Princess NS Gr. 1-3
SSR1-11	Passion of Jesus: A Play Gr. 7-8
SSA1-12	Passport to Adventure Gr. 4-5
SSR1-06	Passport to Adventure Gr. 7-8
SSR1-04	Personal Spelling Dictionary Gr. 2-5
SSPC-29	Pets B/W Pictures
SSE1-03	Phantom of the Opera Gr. 7-9
SSN1-171	Phoebe Gilman Author Study Gr. 2-3
SSY1-06	Phonics Gr. 1-3
SSK1-33	Picture Math Book Gr. 1-3
SSN1-237	Pierre Berton Author Study Gr. 7-8
SSN1-179	Pigman Gr. 7-8
SSN1-48	Pigs in Literature Gr. 2-4
SSN1-99	Pinballs NS Gr. 4-6
SSN1-60	Pippi Longstocking NS Gr. 4-6
SSF1-12	Pirates Gr. 4-6
SSK1-13	Place Value Gr. 4-6
SSB1-77	Planets Gr. 3-6
SSR1-74	Poetry Prompts Gr. 1-3
SSR1-75	Poetry Prompts Gr. 4-6
SSB1-66	Popcorn Fun Gr. 2-3
SSB1-20	Porcupines Gr. 3-5
SSB1-55	Practice Manuscript Gr. Pk-2
SSB1-56	Practice Cursive Gr. 2-4
SSF1-24	Prehistoric Times Gr. 4-6
SSE1-01	Primary Music for Fall Gr. 1-3
SSE1-04	Primary Music for Spring Gr. 1-3
SSE1-07	Primary Music for Winter Gr. 1-3
SSJ1-47	Prime Ministers of Canada Gr. 4-8
SSN1-262	Prince Caspian NS Gr. 4-6
SSK1-20	Probability & Inheritance Gr. 7-10
SSN1-49	Question of Loyalty NS Gr. 7-8
SSN1-26	Rabbits in Literature Gr. 2-4
SSB1-17	Raccoons Gr. 3-5
SSN1-207	Radio Fifth Grade NS Gr. 4-6
SSB1-52	Rainbow of Colours Gr. 4-6
SSN1-144	Ramona Quimby Age 8 NS 4-6
SSJ1-09	Ranching Community Gr. 3-4
SSY1-08	Reading for Meaning Gr. 1-3
SSR1-76	Reading Logs Gr. K-1
SSR1-77	Reading Logs Gr. 2-3
SSN1-165	Reading Response Forms Gr. 1-3
SSN1-239	Reading Response Forms Gr. 4-6
SSN1-234	Reading with Arthur Gr. 1-3
SSN1-249	Reading with Canadian Authors 1-3
SSN1-200	Reading with Curious George Gr. 2-4
SSN1-230	Reading with Eric Carle Gr. 1-3
SSN1-251	Reading with Kenneth Oppel Gr. 4-6
SSN1-127	Reading with Mercer Mayer Gr. 1-3
SSN1-07	Reading with Motley Crew Gr. 2-3
SSN1-142	Reading with Robert Munsch 1-3
SSN1-06	Reading with the Super Sleuths 4-6
SSN1-08	Reading with the Ziggles Gr. 1
SST1-11A	Red Gr. JK/SK
SSN1-147	Refuge NS Gr. 7-8
SSC1-44	Remembrance Day Gr. 1-3
SSPC-23	Reptiles B/W Pictures
SSB1-42	Reptiles Gr. 4-6
SSN1-110	Return of the Indian NS Gr. 4-6
SSN1-225	River NS Gr. 7-8
SSE1-08	Robert Schuman, Composer Gr. 6-9
SSN1-83	Robot Alert NS Gr. 4-6
SSB1-65	Rocks & Minerals Gr. 4-6
SSN1-149	Romeo & Juliet NS Gr. 7-8
SSB1-88	Romping Reindeer Gr. K-3
SSN1-21	Rumplestiltskin NS Gr. 1-3
SSN1-153	Runaway Ralph NS Gr. 4-6
SSN1-103	Sadako & 1000 Paper Cranes NS 4-6
SSD1-04	Safety Gr. 2-4
SSN1-42	Sarah Plain & Tall NS Gr. 4-6
SSC1-34	School on September Gr. 4-6
SSPC-01	Sea Creatures B/W Pictures
SSB1-79	Sea Creatures Gr. 1-3
SSN1-64	Secret Garden NS Gr. 4-6
SSB1-90	Seeds & Weeds Gr. 2-3
SSY1-02	Sentence Writing Gr. 1-3
SST1-07A	September JK/SK
SST1-07B	September Gr. 1
SST1-07C	September Gr. 2-3
SSN1-30	Serendipity Series Gr. 3-5
SSC1-22	Shamrocks on Parade Gr. 1
SSC1-24	Shamrocks, Harps & Shilleaghs 3-4
SSR1-66	Shakespeare Shorts-Perf Arts Gr. 1-4
SSR1-67	Shakespeare Shorts-Perf Arts Gr. 4-6
SSR1-68	Shakespeare Shorts-Lang Arts Gr. 2-4
SSR1-69	Shakespeare Shorts-Lang Arts Gr. 4-6
SSB1-74	Sharks Gr. 4-6
SSN1-158	Shiloh NS Gr. 4-6
SSN1-84	Sideways Stories Wayside NS 4-6
SSN1-181	Sight Words Activities Gr. 1
SSB1-99	Simple Machines Gr. 4-6
SSN1-19	Sixth Grade Secrets 4-6
SSG1-04	Skill Building with Slates Gr. K-8
SSN1-118	Skinny Bones NS Gr. 4-6
SSB1-24	Skunks Gr. 3-5
SSN1-191	Sky is Falling NS Gr. 4-6
SSB1-83	Slugs & Snails Gr. 1-3
SSB1-55	Snakes Gr. 4-6
SST1-12A	Snow Gr. JK/SK
SST1-12B	Snow Gr. 1
SST1-12C	Snow Gr. 2-3
SSB1-76	Solar System Gr. 4-6
SSPC-44	South America B/W Pictures
SSA1-11	South America Gr. 4-6
SSB1-05	Space Gr. 2-3
SSR1-34	Spelling Blacklines Gr. 1
SSR1-35	Spelling Blacklines Gr. 2
SSR1-36	Spelling Blacklines Gr. 3
SSR1-37	Spelling Blacklines Gr. 4
SSR1-14	Spelling Gr. 1
SSR1-15	Spelling Gr. 2
SSR1-16	Spelling Gr. 3
SSR1-17	Spelling Gr. 4
SSR1-18	Spelling Gr. 5
SSR1-19	Spelling Gr. 6
SSR1-27	Spelling Worksavers #1 Gr. 3-5
SSM1-02	Spring Celebration Gr. 2-3
SST1-01A	Spring Gr. JK/SK
SST1-01B	Spring Gr. 1
SST1-01C	Spring Gr. 2-3
SSM1-01	Spring in the Garden Gr. 1-2
SSB1-26	Squirrels Gr. 3-5
SSB1-112	Stable Structures & Mechanisms 3
SSG1-05	Steps in the Research Process 5-8
SSG1-02	Stock Market Gr. 7-8
SSN1-139	Stone Fox NS Gr. 4-6
SSN1-214	Stone Orchard NS Gr. 7-8
SSN1-01	Story Book Land of Witches Gr. 2-3
SSR1-64	Story Starters Gr. 1-3
SSR1-65	Story Starters Gr. 4-6
SSR1-73	Story Starters Gr. 1-6
SSY1-09	Story Writing Gr. 1-3
SSB1-111	Structures, Mechanisms & Motion 2
SSN1-211	Stuart Little NS Gr. 4-6
SSK1-29	Subtraction Drills Gr. 1-3
SSY1-05	Subtraction Gr. 1-3
SSY1-11	Successful Language Pract. Gr. 1-3
SSY1-12	Successful Math Practice Gr. 1-3
SSW1-09	Summer Learning Gr. K-1
SSW1-10	Summer Learning Gr. 1-2
SSW1-11	Summer Learning Gr. 2-3
SSW1-12	Summer Learning Gr. 3-4
SSW1-13	Summer Learning Gr. 4-5
SSW1-14	Summer Learning Gr. 5-6
SSN1-159	Summer of the Swans NS Gr. 4-6
SSZ1-02	Summer Olympics Gr. 4-6
SSM1-07	Super Summer Gr. 1-2
SSN1-18	Superfudge NS Gr. 4-6
SSA1-08	Switzerland Gr. 4-6
SSN1-20	T.V. Kid NS. Gr. 4-6
SSA1-15	Take a Trip to Australia Gr. 2-3
SSB1-102	Taking Off With Flight Gr. 1-3
SSK1-34	Teaching Math with Everyday Munipulatives Gr.
SSN1-259	The Tale of Despereaux NS Gr. 4-6
SSN1-55	Tales of the Fourth Grade NS 4-6
SSN1-188	Taste of Blackberries NS Gr. 4-6
SSK1-07	Teaching Math Through Sports 6-9
SST1-09A	Thanksgiving JK/SK
SST1-09C	Thanksgiving Gr. 2-3
SSN1-77	There's a Boy in the Girls... NS 4-6
SSN1-143	This Can't Be Happening NS 4-6
SSN1-05	Three Billy Goats Gruff NS Gr. 1-3
SSN1-72	Ticket to Curlew NS Gr. 4-6
SSN1-82	Timothy of the Cay NS Gr. 7-8
SSF1-32	Titanic Gr. 4-6
SSN1-222	To Kill a Mockingbird NS Gr. 7-8
SSN1-195	Toilet Paper Tigers NS Gr. 4-6
SSJ1-35	Toronto Gr. 4-8
SSH1-10	Toy Shelf Gr. P-K
SSPC-24	Toys B/W Pictures
SSN1-163	Traditional Poetry Gr. 7-10
SSH1-13	Transportation Gr. 4-6
SSW1-01	Transportation Snip Art
SSB1-03	Trees Gr. 2-3
SSA1-01	Tropical Rainforest Gr. 4-6
SSN1-56	Trumpet of the Swan NS Gr. 4-6
SSN1-81	Tuck Everlasting NS Gr. 4-6
SSN1-126	Turtles in Literature Gr. 1-3
SSN1-45	Underground to Canada NS 4-6